MONIKA WEGLER

My Dwarf Rabbit

BARRON'S

CONTENTS

1 Typical Dwarf Rabbit

2 How Rabbits Like to Live

5 Hygiene and Health Care

6 Learning, Training, and Activities

Family Planning and Raising Young
7

What to Do When There Are Problems
8

Appendix

Typical
Dwarf Rabbit

Incredible, but true: These adorable dwarf rabbits are in
every way the equal of their ancestor, the little wild rabbit,
as well as their large rabbit relatives.

Temperament and Abilities of the Rabbit

If you have chosen dwarf rabbits as your favorite pet and would like to care for them, then you should know everything about the temperament, abilities, and habits of these animals. Only then can you provide a happy life for your dwarfs.

Young dwarf rabbits are simply enchanting and irresistible. With their soft fur and big button eyes, they capture the hearts of one and all; children, especially, want a little bunny to cuddle and love. Who would ever guess, looking at these quiet, gentle creatures, that they also have a snappish side and are not as easy to keep as they are often claimed to be?

These cheerful little animals require lots of exercise, the company of other rabbits, and the opportunity—even indoors—to satisfy their basic needs. All this takes time as well as money. And then there are the little "accidents" that a rabbit lover can best handle with a sense of humor.

Incidentally, once you've seen how a lonely, apathetic caged rabbit blossoms into a happy bunny hopping around cheerfully with his rabbit buddies, you'll never want to keep these pets any other way. In this guide, you'll find many new ideas I've come up with as well as plenty of illustrations that will help you understand your dwarf rabbit even better. My sincerest wish is that both of you—human and rabbit—can be truly happy living together.

A Common Origin

All house rabbits, whether purebred dwarfs weighing scarcely 2 pounds (1 kg) or Flemish Giants tipping the scales at 18 pounds (8 kg), are descendants of the European Rabbit (*Oryctolagus cuniculus*). The European Rabbit is native to the barren scrubland of southwestern Europe. To survive there and make do with the meager food supply, rabbits had to develop a special digestive system. Recent scientific studies confirm that our modern dwarf rabbits need a similar diet of plants

Standing up on his hind legs to reach a dandelion leaf is no problem for this five-week-old Mini Lop. ▶

◀ *Easter bunnies and colorfully decorated eggs are a traditional part of Easter. To delight the children, though, it's better to give chocolate bunnies rather than the real thing.*

especially high in crude fiber and rather low in nutritional value to stay fit and healthy. (see Diet, page 63.)

A Little Rabbit History

When Phoenician sailors discovered little gray rabbits living on the Iberian Peninsula more than 3,000 years ago, they soon learned how tasty rabbit meat is. However, they confused the rabbit with the hyrax of their Syrian homeland and named the new land "I-shepan-im," or "Island of the Hyrax." The Romans adopted this misnomer into their language and called the Iberian Peninsula "Hispania," the name we still use today. The Romans kept half-wild rabbits in walled gardens called *leporaria* as a welcome addition to their menu. During the Middle Ages, rabbits were raised primarily by monks in monasteries because, by papal decree, newborn rabbits were considered "meatless" fare and could be eaten during Lent. By the middle of the

sixteenth century, rabbits were available in a wide variety of coat colors and sizes, although they were used primarily for food and fur.

The Emergence of the Breeds

The heyday of rabbit breeding began with the Industrial Revolution after the turn of the century. Hutches were built in city plots and small gardens, and enthusiastic hobbyists joined to form rabbit-breeding clubs. Then as now breeders exhibited their most beautiful animals at rabbit shows where judges evaluated them according to precisely established breed standards and point systems. Today there are about 70 recognized breeds in Europe and 47 in the United States with a wide range of body types, fur lengths, colors, and weight categories. If you include the color varieties into which the individual breeds are subdivided, the number of rabbit breeds runs to several hundred.

Whenever I visit a huge national show with 20,000 animals, I'm always impressed by the tremendous diversity of the breeds.

Rabbits Capture Our Hearts

Because of the close interaction between hobbyists and their rabbits, the animals became more and more tame. Domestication is an important prerequisite for keeping rabbits as pets. And naturally, cute little dwarf rabbits led the rest in capturing our hearts, a conquest that began in the fifties. Today rabbits remain popular as house pets.

The dwarf breeds

The White Netherland Dwarf: When the use of ermine pelts was outlawed at the beginning of the nineteenth century, a substitute was needed. One was found in the "Polish Rabbit," no bigger than a wild rabbit, with pure white fur and red eyes (i.e., albino). The English bred the first dwarfs with these animals in 1884, and in 1918 they arrived in Germany. This makes the White Netherland Dwarf (known in Germany as the *Hermelin*) the oldest dwarf breed. All colored Netherland Dwarf rabbits are descended from the White Netherland Dwarf.

Always alert

▶ **1** **In an open meadow** without cover, the helpless rabbit is at the mercy of its enemies. She has to stay alert—even when eating!

▶ **2** **These two rabbits** take cover by huddling together in high grass. This instinctive behavior is important for "flight animals" like rabbits.

Colored Netherland Dwarfs

These include all dwarfs with colored fur, present either as a uniform body color or as markings. The dwarf breeds are further differentiated according to length and structure of the fur: normal fur as well as fox, jamora, rex, and satin fur.

Dwarf rabbits are among the
most popular pets,
but they are not "easy-care."

Mini Lops

The cute little Mini Lops are, strictly speaking, not "true" dwarfs, but rather have been bred down from Lop rabbits. They don't carry the dwarfing gene (Dw). Mini Lops originated either in Holland or Germany and were exhibited for the first time in 1964. This breed has long droopy ears and, weighing up to 4½ pounds (2 kg), is

The largest and smallest rabbit breeds in comparison: Flemish Giant at 18 pounds (8.0 kg) and White Netherland Dwarf at 2 pounds (1.0 kg).
▼

heavier than the other dwarf breeds (see Breed portraits, pages 26 to 31).

A Comparison of Wild Rabbits and Hares

Rabbits and hares are frequently confused with each other. Upon closer inspection, though, you'll see they don't look at all alike. Nor do they have much in common in other ways. Because they have different chromosome numbers, the two species cannot breed with each other. Nor would Brer Rabbit allow himself to be tamed and kept in a hutch like the rabbit (see Table, right).

Rabbits Gnaw, but They Aren't Rodents

If you watch a rabbit busily chewing everything he comes across, you might be tempted to think that rabbits are rodents. However, zoologists place both the hare (*Lepus*) and the rabbit (*Oryctolagus*) in the order Lagomorpha. "True" rodents move the lower jaw backward and forward with no sideways motion. Lagomorphs, in contrast, grind their food using circular movements of their jaws. And rodents, unlike lagomorphs, can grasp their food with their front feet. When I watch my Freddy as he chews a carrot lying on the floor, and it just won't keep still, I wonder if my little lagomorph wouldn't find it quite useful to be able to hold his food between his front paws. On the other hand, though, lagomorphs are able to stretch and yawn like cats.

THE DIFFERENCE BETWEEN COMMON HARES AND EUROPEAN RABBITS

Common Hare (*Lepus europaeus*)		European Rabbit (*Oryctolagus cuniculus*)
large, slender with long legs	**body type**	small, rather compact
5–5½ inches (12–14 cm), tips laced with black	**ears**	2½–3 inches (6–8 cm)
6½–13 pounds (3–6 kg)	**weight**	3½–5½ pounds (1.5–2.5 kg)
24–28 inches (60–70 cm)	**body length**	16–20 inches (40–50 cm)
earthy reddish brown, belly light	**coat color**	grayish brown, belly light
48	**chromosome number**	44
no	**can be domesticated**	yes
prefers meadows, fields, and forests	**habitat**	prefers dry, sandy soil, hills, open country with plenty of cover
only above ground, digs "forms" (hollows in the earth)	**nesting and kindling sites**	digs underground burrows, where it spends a lot of time
solitary, except during mating season	**social behavior**	social animal, lives in colonies
long-distance runner with lots of stamina, escapes by running away	**escape behavior**	agile sprinter, lacks endurance, escapes into burrows
40–42 days	**gestation period**	28–34 days
1–4 young	**litter size**	3–7 young
precocial = furred, eyes and ears open, independent at a young age	**newborns**	altricial = naked, blind, deaf, very helpless

▶ **1** **Wild rabbits dig** underground tunnels where they take shelter. Our dwarfs are happy, too, if—like Freddy here—they can dig to their heart's content.

▶ **2** **Using his chin gland,** Pumpkin marks a branch. Rabbits communicate with each other using their noses and olfactory signals.

▶ **3** **Standing up on his hind legs** allows a rabbit to reach food even if it's up high. He sniffs the leaf first, then nibbles at it.

How Do Rabbits Like to Live?

Every dwarf rabbit develops a unique personality as a result of his environment and heredity. If you keep several rabbits, you will soon discover this by observing and comparing your rabbits with each other. Furthermore, all rabbits—regardless of origin and breed—have common behavioral patterns that they inherit as part of their genetic makeup. Come with me now as we explore the exciting world of the wild rabbit. Learn to speak "rabbit" and pick up some tips that will help you in your everyday interactions with your dwarf rabbits.

Together and Never Alone

The wild rabbit is a social animal who lives in a family group consisting of several males ("bucks") and females ("does"), up to ten animals on average. Individual groups can merge to form colonies with 100 or more animals. Within the community, there is a strict social hierarchy. Dominant (higher-ranking) does in particular will defend their burrows aggressively during mating season and when raising young. At the onset of sexual maturity, bucks fight fiercely for dominance until one alpha male (leader of the group) emerges victorious. Defeated rivals run away, so serious injuries are avoided (see pages 130/131).

Consequences for pet owners:
▶ Rabbits are social creatures who need others of their kind in order to express their full range of social behaviors.
▶ Animals forced to live alone will pine away and develop behavioral problems.
▶ Learn more about the best way to put together pairs or groups of rabbits as well as everything you need to know about neutering on pages 52 and 85.

In the Shelter of the Burrow

Rabbits are passionate diggers. Anyone familiar with this knows what I'm talking about: countless holes in the flower beds, tunnels dug beneath backyard enclosures . . . In an emergency an indoor rabbit may even try to burrow through the carpet. Why do they do that? Certainly not to annoy us. They are following their natural instincts! Wild rabbits dig full-blown tunnel systems called warrens, which improve their chances of survival.

Refuges: The moment a rabbit sees, hears, or smells something threatening, he warns the others by vigorously thumping his hind legs, and they all disappear in a flash into their underground burrows. Should a predator such as a weasel follow them there, the rabbits can usually escape through one of their many emergency exits. As a short-distance sprinter the rabbit doesn't have the stamina to endure lengthy pursuit by larger predators (e.g., foxes and dogs). For this reason rabbits never go farther than 55 to 220 yards (50–200 m) from the protection of the burrow. Consequently, rabbits are very sedentary animals.

Protection from bad weather: The warren lies two to three yards (2–3 m) below ground, soil conditions permitting. Here the wild rabbits rest in enlarged dens, protected from the

TIP

Nest box in the cage

Sometimes dwarfs fight in their cage. If one of the animals runs into the nest box and is cornered there by the "aggressor" and attacked, panic ensues and the squabbling escalates. For this reason, the nest box should have both an entrance and an exit, like the warrens of wild rabbits.

damp, pleasantly cool during the heat of summer, and comfortably warm when winter moves in with snow and freezing cold.

Consequences for pet owners:

▸ Without safe places to run for cover, a dwarf rabbit feels completely at the mercy of the environment. Open, empty areas without hiding places

▸ The backyard enclosure must be constructed so that it's escape-proof (see page 46). Otherwise your pets will disappear, never to be seen again.

▸ Note that the backyard enclosure potentially subjects your pet to the danger of predators.

Happy at Twilight

Wild rabbits are crepuscular, meaning they are active primarily in the early morning hours and at twilight, but also

DID YOU KNOW THAT . . .

. . . wild rabbits are master tunnelers?

The tunnels in a rabbit warren can total 50 yards (45 m) in length and go as much as 3 yards (3 m) deep. This labyrinth of tunnels full of twists and turns helps the wild rabbits confuse intruders and leap out through steep emergency exits leading straight up to the surface ("bolt holes"). Rabbits dig with their front paws and push the excavated earth away with their hind legs, working as a team above ground and below.

make the animals nervous. For this reason, every cage should have a nest box. Exercise areas, whether indoors, on the balcony, or in the yard, must be equipped with plenty of retreats. If you keep your rabbits outdoors, you need to provide weatherproof shelters and roofs to protect against damp and cold (see pages 41 and 45).

▸ A digging box indoors as well as a sand pile in the outdoor enclosure will delight these enthusiastic tunnelers (see page 102). Here they can dig to their heart's content.

at night. At midday, the animals are quieter. This is true of our dwarf rabbits as well, although unfortunately too many people are unaware of it. Time and again I get letters from rabbit owners who can't sleep because their rabbit scrabbles around like crazy in the cage at night. This is especially disruptive if the cage is in the children's room.

What can you do? You can't simply switch off the animal's internal clock, and the dwarf won't just go to sleep when it suits us.

Dwarf rabbits need plenty of exercise **as pets**. House rabbits living in a cage must have some free-roaming time every day.

Recommendations for pet owners:

▶ Give your dwarfs a large cage, an exercise enclosure, plenty of activities, and lots of free-roaming time as well as interaction with other rabbits so they can let off steam.

▶ Don't put the cage in the bedroom. I keep my animals in a separate room.

Flight and Prey Animals

As so-called prey animals, wild rabbits are eaten by predators such as hawks, foxes, and weasels. This makes them an important part of the ecosystem, even though many people regard them as pests. Escape behavior is inborn in them, as is the constant watchfulness that makes use of all their senses. It's in their nature to take off in a flash at the first sign of danger or to conceal themselves by flattening their bodies against the ground. If you're used to dealing with "predatory" cats or dogs, you'll quickly notice that the behavior of "prey animals" is completely different.

Not a playful animal: You can't really play with rabbits the way you can with dogs or cats, since they have no prey-seeking behavior. You can make their exercise areas interesting and teach your dwarfs little tricks, but don't expect them to go chasing after balls.

An animal to observe: It's fascinating to observe rabbits, and you should be pleased if your dwarf seeks your company of her own accord. No rabbit likes being forced to cuddle, though, or being carried around constantly. Responsible parents explain to children that their bunny is not a toy (see Parents' Extra, page 54).

Rabbits are susceptible to stress: Feeling nervous around your rabbits or suddenly grabbing them from above is stressful for them. As sedentary animals, rabbits are also upset by any new and unfamiliar terrain. For this reason, I don't think it's appropriate to take even the most trusting rabbit for a walk anywhere on a leash or to participate in the popular sport of "rabbit hopping" out in some open field. Unlike dogs, the rabbit doesn't enjoy agility training.

This dwarf rabbit cowers fearfully on the ground.

▼

The Silent Rabbit

To survive in the wild, rabbits must behave as quietly and inconspicuously as possible so that they don't attract predators. If they are sick or injured, the animals retreat to their burrows. This survival strategy is inborn in dwarf rabbits as well. That's why all too often pet owners fail to hear, observe, or properly understand their silent little companions. Here are the rabbit's most important vocalizations:

Contentment: Rabbits make soft grinding noises with their teeth when they're enjoying being petted. This expression of contentment is so soft, though, that you can hear it only if you keep perfectly still.

Pain: Loud tooth gnashing is always a sign of pain. It is usually accompanied by general apathy, a dull, unhappy look, and a tense hunched posture.

Mating: The buck makes deep, throaty humming noises during the mating ritual and after copulation.

Defense: Rabbits always make growling, spitting, and hissing sounds when they are very angry and feel threatened. This warning says loud and clear; "Keep away!" Ignore it and you'll have to reckon with a lightning-quick attack, regardless of whether you're rabbit or human (see page 19).

Annoyance: Grunting tones that come quickly one after another like a kind of grumbling are also expressions of annoyance. Many rabbits grumble if

1 **Nose twitching** is a rhythmic raising of the inner nasal folds that lets the rabbit detect even the faintest scents. Here my red dwarf Pumpkin is sniffing some yarrow.

2 **Rabbit eyes** are located relatively high on the sides of the head and thus allow the animals nearly 360-degree vision, even overhead. This lets them spot enemies—including birds of prey up in the sky—in plenty of time.

The rabbit uses tactile hairs to sense the ▶
width and height of a narrow passageway.

you want to catch them and put them in their cages. I had a doe who mastered this perfectly.

Abandonment: I heard this anxious whimpering only once. Many years ago my doe dropped two of her newborns outside her warm nest, and the dangerously chilled babies whimpered for their lives. This woke me up, and I held the two crying babies against my body to warm them up, then returned them to the protection of their nest.

Mortal terror: Rabbits utter shrill shrieks and screams only when they sense they are in mortal danger. This is usually just before a predator seizes them, but it can also happen if somebody suddenly grabs a timid, frightened youngster who then panics.

Agitation: Drumming, stamping thumps are originally acoustic warning signals for other rabbits: "Look out! Enemy approaching! Run for it!" If the rabbit thumps vigorously with his hind legs on the ground, he's frightened or at least very agitated and tense.

Body Language and Behavior Patterns

In contrast to vocalizations, rabbits have a distinct body language. Mini Lops have a somewhat reduced range of expression because of their drooping ears. If you look closely, though, you'll soon discover the fine distinctions (see photos, pages 30 to 31).

"Periscope bunny"

When a rabbit hears or see something that attracts her attention, she stands up on her hind legs and "tests the wind," as it's called. In this upright position, the "periscope bunny" can have a good look around and is better able to detect scents as well as sounds.

Escape behavior

Vertical leaps, midair turns, and lightning-quick sprints are all part of the lifesaving escape behavior of the wild rabbit. Even the little ones practice in play what will later help them escape an enemy in an emergency: short sprints up to 25 mph (40 km/h) and the ability to twist around 180 degrees in midair! Even dwarf rabbits have certain "wild moments" when they suddenly race around like mad and make aerial leaps and turns. All of this is an expression of pure joy and vitality. Rabbits need this to stay fit and burn up excess energy.

When rabbits relax

You can observe this when your rabbits relax. Don't disturb them during these times:

▸ They are sitting in a relaxed squatting position, ears erect.
▸ They are squatting there chewing quietly, ears back.
▸ They are lying stretched out on their bellies or sides, heads resting on the floor, hind legs stretched out to the back or side.

▸ They are rolling in the sand, an activity that they love.
▸ They are stretching and yawning after a nap, which loosens the muscles and promotes circulation.

Paw scraping and scratching

Rabbits scrape and scratch with their front paws:

▸ Sexually mature bucks, does in heat, and pregnant does often scrabble around restlessly in their bedding.
▸ If they don't have an opportunity to indulge their inborn digging instinct, perhaps in a sand box, rabbits will resort to scratching at the carpet.
▸ Dominant rabbits like to scrape where rivals have placed their scent marks.
▸ If your rabbit paws on your lap, this can also mean, "Please keep petting me."

Circling

During the mating ritual, the male rabbit circles his chosen female. If he circles your legs, he's courting you as if you were a substitute partner.

Hello and good-bye

▸ Among rabbits, gentle nudging with the muzzle is a friendly greeting ritual and indicates a desire for attention.

◂ *Munchkin, my Black Tan Netherland Dwarf, nibbles on a nettle. Did it taste good? You should usually let nettles wilt before feeding them to your rabbit.*

▸ If your rabbit nudges you, this means, "Hello, here I am, pet me."

▸ Energetic shoving means, "Don't bother me!"

▸ Among rabbits, nipping and poking are a sort of bickering that should not be taken too seriously (in contrast to serious biting attacks). If your dwarf nips you, don't immediately cry, "Ouch!" but instead place the animal on the floor and leave him alone.

▸ Ear shaking is also an expression of displeasure that means, "I don't like that."

Social grooming

Rabbits who like each other groom and lick each other's fur. This is known as social grooming because this form of behavior strengthens the bonds of friendship within the group. If your dwarf licks your hand or your arm, usually while you're petting her, it means, "I like you and that's why I'm grooming you."

Camouflage

The rabbit flattens himself on the ground, ears laid back, eyes wide with fear: This is how the wild rabbit camouflages himself when it's too late to escape to the burrow. If your dwarf exhibits this behavior, something has frightened him. Whatever you do, don't run to him frantically, because this can trigger panicky flight (see photo, page 15).

Cautious curiosity

The forequarters and head are stretched far forward, the ears are slightly forward, the hindquarters are raised, the legs are extended (ready to bolt),

and the tail is down. Wary and ever alert, this is how a rabbit approaches if there's something unknown to investigate: unfamiliar terrain, a strange rabbit, a new object. Curious, but not too brave, and always ready to run if danger threatens.

Self-confident or submissive

A self-confident rabbit approaches with the tail erect. This is how dominant rabbits confront other rabbits (see photos, page 121).

A submissive rabbit cowers, as if trying to make herself look small. If she's fearful, her ears are back. If she is showing another higher-ranking rabbit her respect, but without fear, the ears stay up.

If she wants attention, she pushes her head close to the other rabbit, but always keeps her head and body lowered.

Look out! Attack!

The ears are back, the body is tense and stretched forward, ready to attack; there may be a short growl. This means, "Careful! Stay away, or else I'll scratch and bite!"

The World of Scent

All rabbits have well-defined marking behavior that helps them get along in the world and communicate with each other. Rabbits use their chins to rub everything they regard as their property and part of their territory (chinning) (see photo, page 13). The chin glands are under the tongue but release their secretions to the outside through several pores on the underside of the chin. Our noses cannot detect these

Rabbits don't "see" the world the way we do. Their **acute sense of smell** allows them to analyze olfactory messages and so to understand their environment.

olfactory messages. Dominant rabbits, by the way, mark the most intensely, independent of sex. Rabbits feel at home only in surroundings that they have marked. Unfamiliar scents make the animals uneasy. When my Mini Lop Freddy detected the scent of his rival in a room, he thumped the floor vigorously with his hind legs in agitation. Marking with fecal pellets serves to indicate territorial boundaries. With the help of anal glands, the rabbit coats his droppings with a secretion and so leaves his aromatic "calling cards" that say, "My family and I live here. Strangers better respect the boundaries of my territory!" In contrast to the scents from the chin glands, these territorial markers can even be detected by humans because of their intensely sweet, heavy odor.

The inguinal glands, located in the bare folds of skin on either side of the genital openings on the rabbit's underbelly, have the following importance:

Recognize other rabbits: If a rabbit detects another rabbit's scent, he can immediately determine whether or not the other rabbit is a member of the group, what the strange rabbit's sex is, and, if it's a doe, whether she is ready to breed. This "recognition" is so intense that it goes far beyond visual perception. Here's a simple but impressive experiment I carried out to test this behavior: I used a tissue to clean the skin folds of my buck Pumpkin. Then I held the tissue right under the nose of my male Mini Lop Freddy. In a flash he seized the tissue, clawed it furiously, and bit into it. When I repeated the test, but this time used the scent of my doe Mimi, Freddy went into absolute raptures and was ready to mate. And all of this was triggered by scents on a paper tissue without either of the other animals being present. This experience of our little friends' world of scent, so alien to us humans, made quite an impression on me.

Rabbits don't want to live alone. They need the companionship of other rabbits.

▼

Changing the color of the urine: With the inguinal glands, rabbits can even add their unique scent to their urine when necessary and change the color of the urine with different chemical compounds (from pale yellow to reddish orange).

Urine spraying: This is how bucks mark their "chosen one" and dominant animals mark other members of their group. The doe can also spray urine during precopulatory activity; however, this should probably be interpreted as a

The Senses

To survive in the wild, rabbits are equipped with special senses. Sight, hearing, and smell are particularly well developed.

Sight

For a little "flight animal" like the rabbit, early detection of predators

DID YOU KNOW THAT . . .

. . . a rabbit's nose has 100 million olfactory cells?

In comparison to rabbits, our human nose has approximately twelve million olfactory receptor cells. The rabbit picks up scent molecules by rhythmically raising the inner nasal folds. This method of sniffing the air is also called "nose twitching." If a rabbit stands up on her hind legs, she is better able to detect odorants floating around higher up in the air. Rabbit mothers visit their offspring only once a day—and then for only four to five minutes—so that they don't attract enemies. Researchers have found that the newborns, their eyes still closed, can find their mother's life-giving nipples within 15 seconds of waking from sleep. The reflex for this is triggered by a special scent that is produced in the doe's breast and elicits a response from rabbits only and not from any other animal species.

stress reaction. Rabbits also spray urine when in danger—so-called anxiety-induced urination. This happened on my veterinarian's examination table when my doe became frightened and informed us both in no uncertain terms with a well-aimed jet of urine.

coming from any direction is important for survival. The rabbit's sense of sight is designed for this.

▶ The eyes, located relatively high on either side of the head, give the rabbit nearly 360-degree vision, even overhead (see photo, page 16).

MY PET

How keen is your rabbit's sense of smell?

Her olfactory sense is many times more acute than ours. She uses it to test everything that passes in front of her nose, whether it's another rabbit, other animals, or objects. Test your rabbits, alone or as a group, to find how well they react to individual scents.

The test begins:

Preferably at evening, when your rabbits are most active, place one new thing in the exercise area every day (not all together—otherwise the scents will mingle!). In the space below, record how the individual animals react to the following:

○ A new toy like a cardboard box or fruit crate
○ A toy or stick that a dog has played with
○ A T-shirt you have worn for a while

My test results:

▸ Depth perception is limited at close range. The eyes of the rabbit are designed to see well at a distance and react sensitively to motion stimuli.
▸ The pupils cannot adapt to variations in lighting. On the other hand, this crepuscular animal sees quite well in the dark.
▸ Rabbits don't recognize colors; it's thought that they can distinguish only between red and green.

Consequences for pet owners:

▸ Never grab your dwarf from above without warning. He'll think he's being seized by a bird of prey. Always approach him from the front, preferably at eye level, and avoid sudden movements, even around the cage.
▸ Be careful when the dwarf is running free indoors. The animal has a hard time judging distances in three dimensions, especially close up, and could suddenly run between your legs.
▸ Bright sunlight blinds rabbits, as does suddenly switching on the light in a dark room. Always provide shaded areas and drape the cage at night with a lightweight cloth.

Hearing

The erect ears of the dwarf are built like elongated trumpets and can be swiveled independently of each other. Without moving his head, the rabbit uses his ears to pick up sounds from a 360-degree area. Lop rabbits with their drooping ears have a reduced ability to hear.
Consequences for pet owners:
With their acute hearing, even dwarf rabbits are sensitive to loud noises, especially if they are sudden, unexpected, and shrill. This can trigger escape behavior, and the panicky animal can collide with something and injure himself. For example, never try to whistle for your rabbit as you would for a dog (it sounds like the scream of a hawk). I know of one case where a rabbit in a hutch had a heart attack when someone started using a power saw nearby. Rabbits prefer people who speak to them in a friendly, soft, and rather low-pitched tone of voice.

Smell

If you were to compare humans and rabbits, you could say, "We speak using words; rabbits communicate using scents" (see pages 19 and 21).
Consequences for pet owners:
▶ The rabbit's sensitive olfactory mucosa cannot tolerate dusty hay or straw. Refrain from using strong-smelling household cleaners or heavy perfumes, and don't smoke around your rabbit's living quarters!
▶ During the heating season, you should use a humidifier to improve the extremely dry indoor air for your house rabbits. It will benefit you, too. I also use indoor fountains with a large water surface and cold mist vaporizers.

Taste

The rabbit has taste buds in the mouth and pharynx and can distinguish sweet, sour, bitter, and salty. However, don't rely on your rabbit to recognize poisonous plants and refrain from eating them! (see Internet addresses, page 141.)

These dwarfs feel safe and secure in their leafy tent. It provides shade, and they can nibble on it.
▼

And please don't feed your rabbit chocolate cookies, or give her rabbit snacks loaded with sugar, grains, and nuts. I know rabbits love to nibble these sweet treats, but it will just make them fat and upset their digestive system.

Touch

Rabbits have tactile hairs around the mouth and nose, over the eyes, and on the cheeks. Sensory nerves at the roots of these hairs react to the slightest stimuli. This helps the nearsighted rabbit find his way in tight places, especially in the dark and in the underground tunnels of his warren. The animal also receives tactile stimuli via the skin. That's why the little rascals like to snuggle together and enjoy being petted gently. Never pull on these tactile hairs, cut them off, or tickle the animal.

Rabbits are very active animals. Being allowed to romp about in a spacious backyard enclosure is "heaven on earth" for them.

▼

The Dwarf Breeds

If you want a purebred dwarf rabbit, you can learn about the most popular breeds in the following pages. It shouldn't matter too much, though, if a rabbit is purebred or a mixed breed. One is just as lovable as the other.

So many different kinds of animals are sold as "dwarf rabbits" that you should at least know what a "true" dwarf looks like.

The Dwarf Type

The gene (symbol Dw) responsible for the typical appearance of the dwarf was discovered in the United States at the beginning of the twentieth century. If this gene is homozygous, i.e., double (Dw/Dw), then it is always lethal (= causes death). The result is litters with nonviable Double Dwarfs, called "peanuts." To prevent this, "true dwarf" bucks (Dw/dw) are mated with larger stronger "false dwarf" does (dw/dw). Mini Lops don't carry the Dw dwarfing gene. Instead, these rabbits are bred down from Lop rabbits. In the breed standard, the purebred dwarf is described as follows:
The body is compact and rounded, equally broad from front to back; the legs are short. The head is large in relation to the body, with a broad forehead and well-developed muzzle. The eyes are large and prominent. The ears (ideal length 2 inches [5.5 cm]) are erect and close together. The weight is 2 to 3⅓ pounds (1.0–1.5 kg).

The dwarf breeds

In the next few pages I'll introduce you to the following breeds:
Pages 26 to 27: white and colored Netherland Dwarfs with uniform coat color
Pages 28 to 29: colored Netherland Dwarfs with markings
Pages 30 to 31: hair structure breeds like the Fox, Rex, and Jamora; in addition, two Mini Lops
Tip: Although the Lionhead rabbit is not a recognized breed, it is very popular among dwarf-rabbit owners. Dwarf Teddy, Dwarf Angora, and Cashmere Lop are also not recognized breeds. (Breeds not recognized by the American Rabbit Breeder's Association [ARBA] are indicated by *.)

TIP

Teddy, Dwarf Angora & Co.

If you'd like a ball of fluff like this, you should keep in mind that these dwarf breeds have to be brushed every day and frequently even need to be sheared. Their soft fur tangles easily, bedding gets caught in it, and the fur around the anus can become matted with feces. Excessively long fur around the eyes can lead to irritation and even inflammation.

Netherland Dwarf
Blue-eyed White

Weight: 2½ to 3 pounds (1.1–1.35 kg) ideal (from 2 to 3⅓ pounds [1.0–1.5 kg])
Body: Short, compact, rounded, equally wide from front to back, hindquarters well rounded.
Head: Large in relation to body, short with broad forehead and muzzle, broad nose.
Ears: Close together, well-rounded tips, well furred.
Ear length: 2 inches (5.5 cm) ideal (from 1¾ to 2¾ inches [4.5–7 cm])
Fur: Short, dense, soft; guard hair: fine and even.
Fur color: Pure white in both surface and undercolor.
Eye color: In Ruby-eyed (albinos) a ruby glow; in Blue-eyed, blue.
Toenail color: Colorless (white).

Netherland Dwarf
Chinchilla

Weight, body, head, ears, ear length, fur: Corresponds to the standard description for the White Netherland Dwarf.
Fur color: The surface color is pearl white, caused by black guard hairs protruding through the black and white surface fur. The margins of the ears are trimmed (= laced) with black. Underside of the tail and surface color of the belly are white. The young are dark slate blue when born, with the chinchilla color becoming apparent after about 14 days. The fur color corresponds to that of the larger rabbit breed Chinchilla and the animal of the same name.
Eye color: Brown.
Toenail color: Dark brown.

Netherland Dwarf
Chocolate

Weight, body, head, ears, ear length, fur: Corresponds to the standard description for the White Netherland Dwarf.
Fur color: The surface color is a rich dark brown without gray mealiness or white hairs and extends over the entire body. The deeper and glossier the dark brown, the better. The undercolor of the coat is blue to the base of the hair shaft. Can be seen only by blowing into the fur or stroking it forward toward the head. The fur color corresponds to the medium-size rabbit breed Chocolate Havana and the Oriental cat breed of the same name.
Eye color: Brown with a slight ruby glow.
Toenail color: Dark horn colored.

Red Netherland Dwarf
Red

Weight, body, head, ears, ear length, fur: Corresponds to the standard description for the White Netherland Dwarf.
Fur color: The surface color is deep red, glossy. Eye circles, jawline, belly color, inside of the legs, and underside of the tail can be lighter, but not pure white. The undercolor should be as similar as possible to the surface color.
The Red Netherland Dwarf always reminds me of a fox. The fur color corresponds to the medium-size rabbit breed Red New Zealand.
Eye color: Brown.
Toenail color: Dark horn color.

Netherland Dwarf
Agouti

Weight, body, head, ears, ear length, fur: Corresponds to the standard description for the White Netherland Dwarf.
Fur color: Recognized agouti varieties are chestnut, chinchilla, lynx, opal, and squirrel. The fur is similar to that of wild rabbits and hares, with the individual hairs having alternating bands of light and dark. In agouti varieties: dark shading on the back, lighter color on chest and sides; ears laced with black. Belly, insides of the legs, jawline, and underside of the tail white. In Chestnut Agouti, the surface color is reddish brown. The undercolor is always bluish.
Eye color: Brown.
Toenail color: Dark horn colored.

Netherland Dwarf
Black

Weight, body, head, ears, ear length, fur: Corresponds to the standard description for the White Netherland Dwarf.
Fur color: The surface color is deep black and glossy with no rusty tinge or light spots. The undercolor is dark blue. This Black Netherland Dwarf presents a real challenge for me as a photographer. To get the marvelous blue sheen in the jet black fur, you'll need to use an extra fill-in flash. The fur color corresponds to the medium-size rabbit breeds Black Viennese* and Alaska.*
Eye color: Brown.
Toenail color: Dark brown to black.

Netherland Dwarf
Dutch, Blue

Weight, body, head, ears, ear length, fur: Corresponds to the standard description for the White Netherland Dwarf.
Markings: Body color white with colored markings. The body markings cover the hindquarters up to the white "foot stops." On the head the marking color includes the ears and continues over the cheeks to the neck, surrounding the eye and framing the nose. Color varieties are white with black, blue, gray, Thuringer, orange, chocolate, squirrel, and chinchilla.
Eye color: Dark brown.
Toenail color: Colorless (white) in all color varieties.

Netherland Dwarf
Himalayan, Black

Weight, body, head, ears, ear length, fur: Corresponds to the standard description for the White Netherland Dwarf.
Markings: Snow white with black mask that covers only the nose; black ears and black "boots." The tail has a pure, rich color. The markings are purest in winter (cold-induced darkening). In the Blue Himalayan Netherland Dwarf the markings are blue on a white body color. The markings correspond to those of the small-size rabbit breed Himalayan.
Eye color: As in the albinos, glowing ruby red.
Toenail color: Brown.

Netherland Dwarf
Tan, Black

Weight, body, head, ears, ear length, fur: Corresponds to the standard description for the White Netherland Dwarf.
Markings: The surface color of each corresponds to the Tan pattern varieties Black, Blue, and Chocolate; the tan markings are sharply demarcated and cover the nostrils, jowls, eye circles, inside of the ears, inside of the legs, chest, and belly. Markings correspond to those of the small-size rabbit breed Tan.
Eye color: Brown; in Blue Tan it is dark blue gray.
Toenail color: Dark brown.

Netherland Dwarf
Thuringer

Weight, body, head, ears, ear length, fur: Corresponds to the standard description for the White Netherland Dwarf.
Markings: A light reddish yellow surface color with dark guard hairs that are evenly distributed over it like a sooty veil (chamois color). The mask, ears, and legs are a dark sooty color, which gradually fades to the body color. A broad sooty band runs along the sides and hind legs. The markings are like those of the medium-size rabbit breed Thuringer.*
Eye color: Brown.
Toenail color: Dark horn color.

Netherland Dwarf
Silver Marten, Black

Weight, body, head, ears, ear length, fur: Corresponds to the standard description for the White Netherland Dwarf.
Markings: Body color corresponds to that of the color varieties black, blue, or chocolate. It covers the entire body and is interspersed with white-tipped guard hairs. Belly, inside of the legs, underside of the tail, eye circles, jawline, nostrils, and ears are always white. The markings correspond to those of the medium-size rabbit breed Silver Marten.
Eye color: Brown; bluish gray in blue animals.
Toenail color: Dark.

Netherland Dwarf
Broken, Tricolor

Weight, body, head, ears, ear length, fur: Corresponds to the standard description for the White Netherland Dwarf.
Markings: Body color is white. The body markings consist of the spine stripe and the side spots, which are distributed over the flanks and legs on both sides, six to eight spots on each side. Markings on the head include the so-called "butterfly," eye circles, cheek spots, and ear markings. The Tricolor Broken Netherland Dwarf shown here is very difficult to breed and a real rarity.
Eye color: Brown.
Toenail color: Colorless (white).

Dwarf Fox*
Havana

Weight, body, head, ears, ear length: Corresponds to the white and colored Netherland Dwarfs.

Fur: The Dwarf Fox rabbit is a longhair dwarf breed. Its fur is 2 to 2½ inches (5–6 cm) long, with shorter fur on the ears and legs. This dwarf has a dense underwool, which is supported by coarse guard hairs. For this reason, the fur of the Dwarf Fox rabbit, unlike that of other longhair dwarfs, does not have a tendency to mat.

Color: White or havana.

Eye color: Brown; ruby or blue in white animals.

Toenail color: Dark; colorless in white animals.

Mini Rex
Red

Weight, body, head, ears, ear length: Corresponds to the white and colored Netherland Dwarfs. Because of the unique hair structure, individual markings appear more distinctly here.

Fur: In this shorthair breed the individual hairs stand upright, may not be curly, and are only ½ to ⅔ inch (14–17 mm) long. If you stroke the fur toward the head, the hairs remain erect and only gradually return to the natural position.

Fur, eye, and toenail color: As in the larger Rex rabbit varieties, for example the Self Rex, the Broken Rex, and most familiar of all, the Castor Rex.

Mini Lop
Sable Point

Weight: Ideally 3 pounds (1.4 kg) (from 2¼ to 4½ pounds [1.0–2.0 kg]).

Body: Short, compact, wide shouldered, and well muscled.

Head: Corresponds to the Lop type, bridge of the nose arched (Roman nose), broad forehead, and muzzle.

Ears: Horseshoe shaped with the ear openings toward the head. At the base of the ears is a ridge (called the crown) reminiscent of a ram's horns. Ear length is 9½ to 11 inches (24–28 cm).

Fur: Medium in length and dense with abundant guard hair.

Fur, eye, and toenail color: Corresponds to the recognized color varieties. Sable Point: body color cream with darker mask, tail, ears, and legs. Streaks on the back, shading on the hind legs and shoulders.

Mini Lop
Broken, Gray

Weight, body, head, ears, ear length, fur: See standard description, page 30 (bottom). In Holland and England so-called Mini Lops are bred that weigh less (maximum weight 3½ pounds [1.6 kg]) and have shorter ears (8¼ to 10¼ inches [21–26 cm] long; always measured from ear tip to ear tip).
Fur color: Chest, legs, and belly are white, as are the lower jaw and the jawline. There should be a white spot in the middle of the forehead. Head, crown area, lop ears, as well as body are covered by the gray (agouti) broken pattern. Mini Lops also come in other colors.
Eye color: Brown.
Toenail color: Colorless (white).

Jamora*
Harlequin

Weight: 3⅓ to 4½ pounds (1.5–2.0 kg)
Body: Compact, rounded.
Head: Broad, massive, set close to the body.
Fur: Of equal length over the entire body (2 to 2⅓ inches [5–6 cm]). Head, ears, and legs are normally furred. The underwool is very dense, the guard hairs fine like angora with no tendency to mat.
Fur color: Orange with black markings. The dark color should be distributed over both sides of the body in bands or areas of color. Head and ear markings are black and orange or black and orange brindled.
Eye color: Brown.
Toenail color: Corresponds to the toe color of the legs.

Lionhead*
Dwarf Rabbit

This rabbit is not an ARBA-recognized breed that is bred according to a standard.
Weight: Maximum of 3⅓ pounds (1.5 kg).
Body, head, ears, ear length: Corresponds as nearly as possible to the dwarf type (see White Netherland Dwarf, page 26).
Fur type: The characteristic trait of this rabbit is the lionlike mane, which varies considerably in appearance. (photo: the short type). Other rabbits have longer fur on the head (about 4 inches [10 cm] long) as well as on the flanks and chest. On the rest of the body the fur should be of normal length (about ¾ inch [2 cm]). The fur of this dwarf rabbit is easy to care for. Unfortunately, this is not the case for angora hybrids.

How Rabbits Like to Live

The companionship of other rabbits, a safe and secure home with places to hide, plenty of exercise, and a stimulating play area make dwarf rabbits happy.

A Dream Home for Dwarf Rabbits

To create a cozy home for your dwarf rabbits, you first have to understand the temperament of the animals. You'll soon realize that these little creatures make big demands when it comes to their housing as pets.

Before you get a dwarf rabbit, you should think about where you would like to keep her: exclusively indoors, outside in the yard, or inside with occasional fresh-air outings to the yard or balcony in the summer.

Indoor Housing

Many pet owners don't have a house with a yard but would still like to keep a dwarf rabbit as a pet. Do you want the best for your little friend? Here's some good advice on providing the most rabbit-friendly conditions indoors.

The ideal cage

Pet supply stores offer a variety of models, usually consisting of a plastic tray and a removable wire top.
Cage size: For two dwarf rabbits, you need a cage with a minimum floor space of 48 x 24 inches (120 cm x 60 cm) or an extra-large cage measuring about 57 x 32 inches (145 cm x 80 cm). If you have problems cleaning and handling the large tray—I know this from my own experience—you can combine two cages to make a multi-level condo (see page 34).
Bottom tray: A tray depth of 6⅓ to 7

inches (16–18 cm) is more than enough to keep the dwarf from kicking the bedding out of the cage. If the bottom tray is too deep (10 inches [25 cm]), your bunnies won't be able to see out.
Wire cage top: It should have horizontal bars on which the rabbits can stretch and support themselves. Because rabbits sometimes chew on the cage wires, galvanized wire is preferable to plastic-coated. Choose a cage with a swinging door on the front so the rabbits can hop in and out by themselves. There should also be two doors in the cage roof to make it easier for you to work inside. When you're

A chewing log with healthful treats motivates the dwarfs to work for their food. It's fun and it keeps them fit.

◀ *This two-story condo offers the dwarfs plenty of opportunity for exercise.*

perches, houses, and ramps are not made of plastic: If the rabbits chew on them, it could be harmful to their health! Multilevel aviaries made of aluminum are sturdy, but should be constructed so that the litter trays don't make a racket when you're cleaning and handling them. That startles the rabbits. **Homemade:** If you're good at making things, you can find many interesting suggestions for multilevel rabbit condos on Internet forums. Just don't get carried away by the great ideas, though; be sure you also keep practicality in mind. Rabbits like to mark their perches and leave their droppings everywhere, not just in the litter box or bedding. For this reason, you should be able to remove and clean as many of the cage furnishings as possible.

As the bunnies hop and jump around in the cage, they particularly enjoy kicking the bedding out into the room. A bottom tray with high sides (about 6–7 inches [16 to 18 cm]) prevents this. Or you can cover the lower part of the wire mesh walls with a strip of Plexiglas (about 7 inches [18 cm] high).

It's easy for young, inexperienced dwarf rabbits to fall off steep open ramps or unprotected perches high up in the air (3 feet [1 m]) and get hurt.

Rabbits don't like it when bedding from "upstairs" falls on their heads or in their eyes. Bear all this in mind when you start building your dwarfs a "dream mansion."

shopping for a cage, make sure that there are about 8 inches (20 cm) between the nest box and the roof of the cage so the dwarfs can sit there comfortably.

Tip: I advise against plastic hoods because they don't let in enough fresh air.

Multilevel condo

As an alternative to the cumbersome extra-large cage, you can offer your dwarf rabbits a multilevel condo. By adding levels, you give the animals much more room to exercise as well as more variety. They can hop upstairs and downstairs, enjoy the raised perch up above, or retreat to a hiding place down below when necessary. If you buy a ready-made condo, make sure the

The two-story dream home

This model consists of two cages, 48 inches (120 cm) long, 24 inches (60 cm) wide, and 18 inches (45 cm) high, placed one on top of the other. To allow the rabbits access to the top floor, remove the door in the roof of the lower cage and cut out a hole of the same size in the bottom tray of the upper cage. The furnishings are made of untreated pine, can be removed individually, and can easily be scrubbed under hot water. The tunnel leading upstairs with its roof-top observation deck and ground floor support are all absolutely safe even for very small rabbits, and are fitted so exactly that no dirt or bedding can fall from above. To keep the cages from slipping, fasten them together securely with four 12-inch (30 cm) bungee cords (see photos, page 34 and below). I have been using this condo for almost a year and recommend it highly. My dwarf rabbits love this cage, too, even mothers with their babies.

Why Location Is So Important

Unfortunately, the question of where to place the rabbit cage and adjoining exercise area often gets too little attention. This results in constant stress for the animals, who react by developing behavioral and health problems.

Your rabbit's home should be in a quiet, well-lighted, airy spot, not in some dark

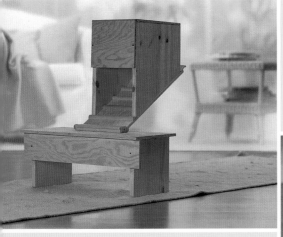

2 **View** of the upper level of the cage with tunnel over the ramp. It serves as an additional observation deck and is designed to keep bedding from dropping on the heads of dwarf rabbits staying downstairs.

▼

1 **Ramp and tunnel** with ground floor support. This sturdy, removable wooden structure lets even young rabbits climb up stairs safely.

corner, but also not in bright sunlight. Rabbits are sensitive to heat. The optimal temperature of their environment is 64°F (18°C). However, they are even comfortable at a room temperature of about 72°F (22°C). With their sensitive hearing, the animals can't stand loud noises like blaring music, shouting, or slamming doors.

Placing the cage in a bedroom can lead to problems since all rabbits are crepuscular (active at dawn and dusk) and nocturnal (active at night) (see page 14).

If you want to prevent respiratory diseases as well as eye inflammations in your rabbits, don't place the cage directly on a cold stone floor or in a draft; also avoid areas where people smoke constantly, or where it's hot and dry when the heat is turned on. I use indoor fountains and humidifiers (cold mist vaporizers) in my house, and they're good for me, too.

These little "flight animals" find themselves in a constant state of stress when they sit defenselessly in their wire cage as two-legged giants rush back and forth far above their heads. For this reason, the little burrow dwellers definitely need a shelter in which they feel safe and secure (see page 126).

Tip: For very shy animals, it helps to put the cage in an elevated spot, perhaps on a table. This solution has some disadvantages, though. Whenever the dwarfs have free-roaming time, you have to pick them up to take them out of the cage or put them back in, and many rabbits really dislike that. Then there's the danger that a squirming bunny will fall when you're carrying him, and get hurt. For this reason, I recommend the "two-story dream home" (see page 34/35 or my solution on page 127).

Perfectly Furnished

Every rabbit home needs certain basic furnishings. Ideas for accessories that also encourage activity are discussed in detail in Chapter 6, beginning on page 102.

Food bowls: I recommend heavy stoneware or ceramic bowls that the rabbits cannot easily tip over or gnaw. A bowl with a diameter of 6 inches (15 cm) allows two animals to eat at the same time. If the bowl is placed directly on the floor, everything will be contaminated too quickly with bedding. To prevent this, I've been setting it on a

◀ *Small rabbit summerhouse with exercise pen and suggested furnishings. This enclosure is suitable only for spending a few hours outdoors (see Suppliers, page 142).]*

block of aircrete (autoclaved aerated concrete) 2¾ inches (7 cm) thick (see photo, page 70).

Water bottle: Rabbits must have water freely available at all times. Gravity water bottles with ballpoint drinking tubes are hung outside on the cage wires and protect the water from contamination. They are practical, but also have their disadvantages. If the drinking tube is not cleaned carefully, germs can lodge there. In addition, they force the rabbit to keep her neck bent at an unnatural angle when drinking. For this reason, I've gone back to giving my rabbits water in a stoneware bowl, which I also place on the aircrete block (see photo, page 70). If I offer the animals both variations, they usually prefer drinking from the bowl, even if they had been accustomed to drinking from the water bottle.

Hay rack: Hay is the rabbit's "daily bread" and is best offered in a rack. Wire hay racks that are hung inside the cage present a slight risk of injury, though. Young dwarfs, in particular, like to jump into them, and their legs could get stuck in the wires. The best solution is to cover the top of the rack with a wooden shelf. A good alternative is a plastic rack (see photo, page 75). Hung on the outside, it doesn't take up space in the cage, and the dwarfs can easily pull the hay through the wires to the inside.

House: Rabbits need a nest box to feel safe and secure in their cage (see page 13). When you're shopping for one, make sure it's large enough, is made of

wood, and has at least two entrances (see Tip, page 13). Contented rabbits like to lie on top of their nest boxes, too, so it should have a flat roof. Plastic houses are not suitable: The rabbits chew on them.

TEST

Are Rabbits Right for Me?

Dwarf rabbits are not low-maintenance pets. That's why you should take this test to see if rabbits are right for you

	Yes	No
1. Do you enjoy observing animal behavior?	○	○
2. Can you stay calm if something gets soiled or nibbled?	○	○
3. Are you prepared to offer your rabbits adequate space for housing and an exercise area?	○	○
4. Are you aware that rabbits are not cuddly pets or toys?	○	○
5. Are you patient and tolerant of other lifestyles?	○	○

ANSWERS: 5 "yes": Excellent prospects for a harmonious life together. Dwarf rabbits will feel right at home with you if you also pay attention to a healthful diet and proper care. 3 to 4 "yes": Perhaps you can give some more thought to the questions you answered with "no." Fewer than 3 "yes": Dwarf rabbits aren't the right pet for you.

Bedding and litter: Dust-free absorbent products such as pellets made from straw, corncobs, wood, and hemp are now available. I have tested all of them, but keep coming back to my old bedding mixture. On the cage floor I put a layer about 2 inches (5 cm) thick of small-animal bedding made from hardwood shavings. Softwood shavings may contain phenols that could be

absorbent straw pellets. A corner litter pan with plastic hood takes up a minimum of space. Watch your dwarfs, however, to be sure they don't chew on it, or you'll have to remove it immediately. I've done away with the litter box in my cage, since my animals use it primarily for digging and sleeping. Now I use litter boxes only in the exercise pen. On the other hand, I clean out the "toilet corner" in the cage every day. Test for yourself which method your dwarfs prefer.

DID YOU KNOW THAT . . .

. . . rabbits like plenty of activity?

If the animals get little or no free-roaming time and exercise, there will be dire consequences: The rabbits become obese, their muscles atrophy, their cardiovascular systems are weakened, and then their life expectancy declines. Joyless existence in a cage also affects their quality of life. Without stimulation and exercise, rabbits become either apathetic or aggressive.

harmful to a rabbit. Straw or towels would be appropriate bedding materials. Also stay away from clumping litter. Wheat, oat, fiber-based, and paper-based litters can all be safely used.

Tip: Don't use cat litter. If an animal ingests it, it can lead to severe digestive problems or even death.

Litter box: Rabbits are usually so clean that they'll choose a specific spot in the cage to use as a toilet area. That's where you can place a plastic tray filled with

Hopping to Their Heart's Content

Allowing dwarf rabbits to run free indoors holds all sorts of dangers (see Table, page 104). Not everyone can make their home completely rabbit-proof. Still, dwarf rabbits want to jump around, dig, chew, and mark their territory. Many can't be litter-box trained as easily as a cat, either. Thus it seems that annoyance is inevitable: a hole in the expensive Persian carpet,

Make sure your indoor rabbits get time to run loose **outside the cage** every day. Plenty of exercise and a change of scenery will do your dwarfs good.

gnawed baseboards, a puddle on the couch, or dismay when the stereo, computer, or telephone suddenly malfunctions because your little nibbler has quietly chewed through the wires. If you don't want to punish your pet by incarcerating him, you can either redesign a separate area as a rabbit room or else set up an enclosure for your animals (see photo, page 40).

A "playpen" for your dwarfs

Your dwarfs can romp around here without constant supervision.
Flooring: Lay down a waterproof tarp on the floor of the room. Over this put a thick layer of newspaper to absorb any urine that soaks through. A chewable straw mat (inexpensive, available at home improvement centers) makes a good "rabbit meadow." If your dwarfs are little "slobs" who leave their droppings everywhere, you can also use durable, easily cleaned wall-to-wall carpeting as the top layer. Please be sure to buy the carpet as a single piece and pull the outer edges beneath the enclosure fence to the outside so that they offer no point of attack for those incisors (mats, individual tiles, or terry cloth are not suitable!).
Fencing: Now combine the condo or several cages with a small-animal exercise pen (from the pet supply store) to make a large run. My enclosure consists of eight galvanized wire fencing panels linked together (see photos,

pages 36 and 46). The door, installed somewhat off the ground, makes it easier for you to climb in without allowing the bunnies to escape. Depending on how you combine the cage with the panels and the wall of the room, you can get a play area measuring 3½ to 6½ yards² (3–5.5 m²). To let your rabbits have the run of the whole house, simply open one fence panel. And one more tip: Place a low cage on the floor against the wall of the room; otherwise it will be used as a "springboard" out of the enclosure. Lay a thick cotton blanket on the roof of the

This willow bridge allows the dwarf to climb in and out of the cage safely.

▼

cage so that the rabbits don't get caught in the bars and hurt themselves when they jump up on it.

Make your layout interesting: Here are a few more suggestions for furnishing your play yard. You'll find additional ideas in Chapter 6 beginning on page 102.

▸ As a digging box use a cat-litter pan with a rim filled with play sand or a mixture of sand and soil (no pre-fertilized garden soil!)

▸ From the pet supply store: willow bridges, cork tubes (to crawl through, hide in, climb on)

▸ From the garden or woods: a log (elevated perch)

▸ My chewing log: encourages the bunnies to stretch up for healthful treats

▸ Wicker basket planted with grass, dandelions, or herbs

You can use wire fence panels to design an indoor play yard with free access to the cage. This way you can offer your dwarfs plenty of exercise and variety.

▼

The Great Outdoors

Rabbits love spending time outdoors. Not only does it stimulate all their senses, but fresh air and exercise also strengthen their immune systems. You can create an outdoor oasis for your pets.

Before your rabbits can romp around outside to their heart's content, you need to make a few preparations. Whether on the balcony or in the yard, simply opening the door and letting the rabbits out is not the best solution.

Small Balconies

You can either give your dwarf rabbits an additional exercise area or build them a winter-proof permanent residence on your balcony.

Location: A balcony that faces east, southeast, or southwest is ideal. A south-facing balcony will quickly overheat in the summer, even in the shade. The windward side (north, northwest), on the other hand, is almost always too damp and usually too drafty.

Safety: Rabbits can slip through even the smallest spaces and have been known to jump over a railing. For this reason, the balustrade must be rabbit-proofed wherever there are gaps, especially close to the floor but also higher up. The best thing to use for this is galvanized wire mesh, ⅔ x ⅔ inch (17 x 17 mm). This stands up to rabbit teeth and will even protect animals on a ground-floor balcony from marauding weasels. Nylon cat netting is unsuitable.

Protection from the sun: Rabbits are very sensitive to heat and absolutely must have an airy spot in the shade. An awning or large beach umbrella works nicely. A piece of canvas can also provide good shade; stretch it from the balustrade to the window ledge, for example, using bungee cords. The cloth should cover about a third of the floor space available to the dwarfs. Always be aware of the changing position of the sun!

Protection from rain: If your balcony doesn't have a roof overhead, you'll have to provide a secure roof for the shelter. A brief period of rain makes little difference to a healthy rabbit, but

---

TIP

Rabbit hutch for the balcony

Hutch: 48 inches (120 cm) long, 24 inches (60 cm) wide, 20 inches (50 cm) high. Material: ¾-inch (18 mm) pine boards. Floor/interior: 6 inches (15 cm) high (paint with asphalt roof paint so urine doesn't penetrate so quickly). Use galvanized wire mesh (⅔ x ⅔ inch [17 x 17 mm]) for the hutch door. To protect against drafts: Place the hutch on 8-inch (20 cm) high wooden legs.

even the most robust animal can't tolerate sitting in the rain for long periods.

Flooring: Balconies with concrete or tile floors are slippery and cold. For this reason, you should lay straw mats on the floor of the roofed rain-proof area or else build an enclosure that can be covered with bark mulch or straw pellets.

Furnishings: Along with the shelter (see Tip, page 41) you should have the following accessories in the balcony enclosure: food and water bowls, litter box, digging box, elevated perches, tunnel, bridges, additional huts (see decorating ideas in the photos, pages 43, 44/45, 103, 111).

Size of the exercise area: Bigger is naturally better. Seven square yards (6 m²) would be the minimum size for long-term housing for two dwarf rabbits. You can enlarge smaller balconies in warm weather by providing access to your indoor living area. This way your rabbits will still feel like part of the family.

Climate change: Animals that have been kept exclusively indoors must be acclimated slowly and carefully. You can put the dwarf rabbits outside in spring when the temperature stays above 54°F (12°C) even at night. Taking indoor rabbits out of their cage in winter and putting them out on the cold balcony for exercise poses a tremendous health risk because these animals have not developed a protective winter coat indoors where it's nice and warm. After a period of acclimation the dwarf rabbits can live on the balcony from spring until fall with no problem.

Trips to the Backyard

Every time my rabbits are allowed to run around in our small backyard, they seem to undergo a transformation. The little rascals really blossom and perform the most amazing leaps. They act like this even though they're allowed to roam free in their own 24-yard² (20 m²) room all day long. There's probably just no substitute for the great outdoors. Of course, I don't just let my little ones run around free in the yard. That would be much too dangerous. I set up a movable outdoor enclosure for them (see photos, pages 36 and 46) and put in some furnishings to make it interesting, and then we all enjoy the gorgeous summer weather together for a few hours.

Movable Outdoor Enclosure

These runs are meant to be used only for a few hours at a time with supervision. They offer absolutely no protection against tunneling or enemies from outside, nor are they suitable for housing your pets overnight or for longer periods! Nevertheless, I recommend them if you have a backyard but can't build a permanent outdoor enclosure. In any case, the fresh air will do your dwarfs good.

▸ Place the enclosure close to the house so that you can keep an eye on your pets.

▸ A tree provides natural shade, although you can't ignore the changing position of the sun.

▸ The enclosure can be set up in just a few minutes and is easily moved to other locations. This is a definite

▲

This balcony enclosure with a shelter for two dwarf rabbits was designed to provide lots of variety.

advantage, because then your dwarf rabbits always have fresh, juicy, unsoiled grass to nibble.

▸ If you combine two enclosures as shown in the photo on page 46, the rabbits get a pen measuring 6 yards² (5 m²) (can be expanded to 12 yards² [10 m²]).

▸ The pen can be anchored solidly in the ground using the metal pins and ground stakes that come along with it, and it can be protected from above with a net.

Tip: Because I always keep my rabbits in view, I prefer not to use a net. Leaping rabbits have been known to get tangled in the net! Smaller enclosures can be covered with wire mesh stretched over a wooden frame.

Rabbit-friendly furnishings

Time and again I see absolutely pitiful dwarf rabbits sitting in a mini-enclosure in the middle of the yard. There are usually no furnishings at all to speak of, just a bowl in one corner of the "play yard"—and that's it! The dwarf doesn't have a little house to protect him from sun and rain or anything else to provide him with stimulation. Then these rabbit owners are surprised that their dwarf doesn't seem to enjoy being outdoors in the fresh air. On the contrary, the animal can even suffer a heatstroke from too much sun and meet an untimely end in the pen (see Heatstroke, page 91).

▸ 1 **A weatherproof hutch** with small exercise pen, both of which are movable and can be used for a few hours of fun out in the yard. The pen can be further enlarged by using wire fence panels.

▸ 2 **Homemade outdoor enclosure**, escape-proof, intruder-proof, weather-proof, and spacious; a grassy play yard is in front of it.

▸ 3 **Interior view** of the walk-in outdoor enclosure with digging box and raised perches for the dwarf rabbits.

Even a small movable outdoor enclosure can be designed to offer plenty of variety. See how in the photo on page 36.

Of course, you can make a roomy enclosure even more interesting (see photo, page 46).

All furnishings are made of natural materials. You can buy wooden huts and cork tubes at a pet supply store. The hollow log has been in continuous use for seven years and is indestructible. I found it in the woods and scraped out the soft, rotten center.

The bench comes from the garden center, as does the landscape edging. I used it to make the bridge between the two enclosures in the photo on page 46. You can also use this flexible chain of split wooden posts to make a natural room divider in the outdoor enclosure (see photo, page 111).

The biggest hit with my rabbits, however, is the tent made from two woven wicker trellises (see photo, page 111). The dwarfs feel safe and secure under this "roof" and enjoy its airy shade even in midsummer.

More new ideas for you to copy are the "hanging bridge" (see Instructions, page 106 and photo, page 103) and my "leafy tepee" (see photo, page 23). The rabbits love to snuggle together under this beech-twig tent and enjoy nibbling on the foliage and branches. After the leaves and twigs have been chewed off, simply replace them with new ones. My dwarfs enjoy it, and it's economical, too. I've found that my animals prefer to use items made of natural materials, which are thus most like their natural surroundings. Maybe you can test this yourself with your next enclosure design and see what your dwarf rabbits have to "say" about it.

Permanent Outdoor Enclosure

If you have the opportunity, you can build your rabbits a bunny-friendly natural habitat. The two photos above show you an attractive example of a permanent enclosure. Before you start, select an appropriate site in the yard. The spot should be partly in sun, partly in shade, and visible from the house so you can keep an eye on it more easily. For two to three dwarf rabbits, plan on a minimum floor space of 7 yards^2 (6 m^2). No question about it: The bigger the enclosure, the better it is for the animals. Think of your own comfort, too, and make sure when you build it that you can enter the enclosure without stooping. Everything should be accessible and easy to clean without acrobatic contortions. Rabbits feel comfortable only in a clean enclosure, and that's the only place they'll remain healthy (see Diseases, beginning on page 83). Naturally, safety plays a major role, too. For the rabbits to live in an outdoor enclosure without danger, they need a sort of security fence that will prevent the animals themselves from escaping as well as protect against intrusion by enemies such as weasels, dogs, or hawks. Rabbits have been known to be stolen, too.

TIP

First outing in spring

When the first tender blades of grass sprout outside in the yard, be careful! Rabbits accustomed to eating little or no green foods are especially likely to pounce on them greedily now, and inevitably they develop serious digestive problems. Get your rabbits used to this fare slowly and carefully before you let them outside.

Here I have combined two movable enclosures consisting of a total of 16 fence panels (32 x 32 inches [80 x 80 cm]) to make an exercise pen measuring 6 yards² (5 m²). The furnishings are made exclusively of natural materials.

Detailed recommendations

As you can see in the photo on page 45, I recommend a full weatherproof roof. This way the floor and furnishings will stay dry even if it rains for days.

Escape-proofing: Rabbits love to dig tunnels—it's in their nature—and they can escape faster than you'd suspect. Burying wire mesh in the ground around the enclosure for protection—even 20 inches (50 cm) deep—doesn't always help. Laying additional wire mesh on the ground provides more security, as do grass pavers. But the animals have so much fun digging in the dirt! Why shouldn't they be able to enjoy it?

That's why I recommend that you dig deeper (about 24 inches [60 cm]), even if this means more work initially. First lay down the grass pavers, which together with the wire mesh sunk in the earth outside the perimeter will prevent escape. Now take the soil you excavated and spread it on the grass pavers. The dwarf rabbits can dig here to their heart's content. The pavers and the wire mesh will stop the little tunnelers, but that doesn't matter: They're still guaranteed to have lots of fun digging.

The substrate: Grass cannot withstand constant use by the animals and is very difficult to clean. Bark mulch should also be avoided. The ideal substrate is children's play sand because you can scoop out the fecal pellets again and again. You can buy this sand, inexpensively packaged in 50-pound (25 kg) bags, in home improvement centers. You could also put down a variety of substrates, perhaps a few stone slabs here and there to wear down the rabbits' toenails and a little corner with some gravel.

Building materials: The most suitable materials are untreated wood and strong wire mesh (15 gauge, ¾ x ¾ inch [1.45 mm, 19 x 19 mm]).

The shelter: In the enclosure shown on the top of page 45, a wooden tool shed (4 yards^2 [3.3 m^2]) was converted and an entrance made to the roofed outdoor enclosure measuring 7½ yards^2 (6.25 m^2). This is a particularly good idea since the straw, hay, food, and pellets can be stored here on a raised platform. If you would like to build a shelter, you can make the one described in the tip on page 41. With a fully roofed outdoor enclosure, a hutch like this is perfectly satisfactory in winter; on warm summer nights the animals can safely sleep outdoors on the benches in their airy enclosure.

Interior design: Here you can use all the suggestions I gave you on page 42 for cage furnishings for a large movable outdoor enclosure.

In addition, I recommend the following for your dwarfs: wooden crates filled with hay to snuggle in, drain pipes to crawl through, tree stumps to use as elevated lookouts, and perhaps a boulder or a pile of rocks to scramble up.

Now all that remains is for your dwarfs to move in. How you welcome them to their new home is the topic of the next chapter.

MY PET

How do your rabbits behave in their play yard?

A new environment is a particularly good place for you to observe how your animals differ from each other in personality and temperament. Are they self-confident and curious, or cautious and hesitant?

The test begins:
- ○ Who is the first to leave the shelter?
- ○ Which rabbit prefers the elevated lookouts?
- ○ Who runs for cover at sudden noises, and who stands up inquisitively on hind legs to investigate?
- ○ Who is the first to try tunneling under the fence?
- ○ Put something new in the enclosure. Who hangs back, and who investigates right away?

My test results:

Welcome Home

Once you have found your dream rabbit, you have to start gaining her trust. If you succeed, nothing will stand in the way of a harmonious life together.

Finding Your Dream Rabbit

Your rabbit's home is ready; all that's missing is the little occupant. Take your time choosing and buying your dwarf rabbit. Spend a while observing the animals before you finally decide on at least two dwarfs.

When choosing and buying a rabbit, feelings play a major role, especially when children are involved. When you make your decision, though, use your head as well as your heart.

Now You're Ready

First of all, make sure nobody in the family is allergic to pet hair. Rabbits can live for eight years or more. That's how long you must take care of your bunnies and, if you have children, share the responsibility as a parent for the animals' welfare (see Parents' Extra, page 54).

Where to find rabbits:

▶ in a pet store
▶ from a breeder
▶ from a private individual
▶ from an animal shelter or animal rescue organization

You can start looking around locally, check the newspaper ads, or search the Internet (see Addresses, page 141). If you're interested in purebred rabbits, you should visit one of the big rabbit shows.

Buyer Beware

You should take plenty of time when buying your pets and pay attention to the following:

Housing: The animals have enough room to move about in the display cage or in their exercise pen. They have plenty of fresh air, water, hay, and good food. Their quarters appear to be clean

Health: Give your chosen candidates a preliminary health check (see Table, page 51). Don't buy an animal from a group in which other rabbits show symptoms of disease.

Rabbits that get along well, like this pair, enjoy snuggling together. ▶

Your dwarfs may have already been infected.

Trust: Regardless of where and from whom you buy your rabbits, if the sellers don't give prospective owners any advice, if they show no interest in the future home of their rabbits and treat them unkindly, don't put your

When choosing a dwarf rabbit, pay attention to temperament. Is the bunny trusting or timid?

trust in these people and don't take any of their rabbits.

Age at purchase: Time and again I see sellers offering dwarf rabbits scarcely more than five to six weeks old, which is far too young to be sold. Unfortunately, part of the blame for this state of affairs falls on buyers who don't want slightly older dwarf rabbits. Yet rabbits who have been separated from their mothers and given up for adoption before they are seven weeks old are more susceptible to disease and

As an alternative to the scruff hold, you can lift a dwarf safely
◀ *like this.*

can develop behavioral problems. For the good of the animals as well as for your own sake, please don't contribute to this problem.

Temperament: If you would like a trusting dwarf rabbit, then pay attention to her behavior when you make your choice. Does she run for the corner of the cage right away, even if you approach quietly and carefully, or does she come over curiously to sniff at your hand? As with many other animal babies, the temperament and behavior of a rabbit are determined by genetic makeup, the behavior of the mother, and the experiences the youngster had during the sensitive early development phase. Affectionate handling right from the start and easygoing, firm-tempered parents are the best guarantee for offspring of the same kind. Nervous, fearful, and very timid animals, on the other hand, need lots of patience, love, and experience before they learn to trust humans (see page 126).

The Advantages of Adult Dwarf Rabbits

Baby rabbits are delightful, no doubt about it. Like all animal babies, though, they are still developing, both physically as well as in their overall personality. In addition, the less you know about the family history of the youngsters, the more surprised you'll be later as their genetic traits are gradually expressed. It's a different story for an adult rabbit. Her character and individual preferences have already developed and are easy to identify. Good animal shelters and other responsible animal rescue organizations are happy to help you choose a rabbit that's right for you.

HOW TO TELL IF A DWARF RABBIT IS HEALTHY

PRELIMINARY HEALTH CHECK

Before you decide on a dwarf rabbit, observe the animal carefully, pick him up in your hands, and check him over.

How to recognize a healthy rabbit:

Behavior:	Cheerful, lively, and responsive to the environment.
Body:	Well muscled. You don't feel any sharp bones protruding. The abdomen is soft; the flanks are not sunken.
Fur:	Glossy, dense, and smooth. In a healthy animal the fur flies back to the original position if you stroke it against the direction of growth. Watch for bald spots or crustiness.
Eyes:	Clear, bright, and open. No cloudiness or discharge. Eyelids are not stuck together.
Nose:	Dry and clean, without discharge. The dwarf isn't sneezing.
Ears:	Clear, no waxy buildup or crustiness. Visible ear movement.
Teeth:	The animal is not drooling. Properly aligned upper and lower pairs of incisors meet in a scissors bite (see photo page 79, Checking the teeth).
Anus:	The anal region is clean, dry, and not smeared with feces.

Tip: Don't buy a dwarf rabbit from stock in which another animal shows signs of disease. Your "dream rabbit" could already be infected. If you get a new animal and want to introduce her to your resident rabbit, you should first have the newcomer checked by a veterinarian.

The companionship of other rabbits is more important than anything else for **little dwarf rabbits**. Only then are they truly happy in our care.

The animals have all been examined by a veterinarian, the bucks are already castrated, and you pay only a small adoption fee. If you choose a pair that is already bonded, you'll have no problems with introductions. A few months ago, I took in a doe that had been given away in a cardboard box together with her newborns. "Mommy" felt at home with me right away and was a devoted mother. Her offspring are the models for the photos in this handbook. You can admire Peter, a particularly bright youngster, on the title page.

I recommend a carrier like this to transport your rabbits safely.

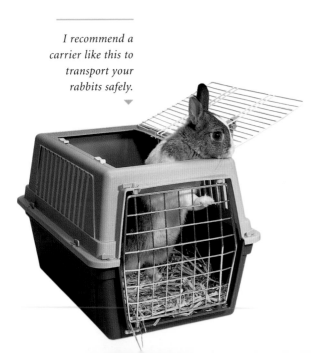

A Lively Group

As I describe in detail in the first chapter, all rabbits are naturally gregarious and need social contact with at least one other member of their species. A person is no substitute for this. That's why it's best to start by choosing two littermates or older animals that are already living together amicably.

A pair: Doe and buck are the ideal combination and almost always get along. Be careful, though: There's a good reason rabbits are regarded as fertility symbols in many cultures. Dwarfs are sexually mature somewhere between the third and fourth months of life. To prevent unwanted offspring, bucks must be castrated at the proper time. Take the buck to your veterinarian when he is 12 weeks old; the vet can then determine the best time for castration, depending on the animal's development (see Neutering, page 85).

Two bucks: They live together harmoniously when they're young. With the onset of sexual maturity, however, bucks start to fight with each other. This behavior is completely natural for rabbits and is how they establish their position in the social hierarchy. If the animals are confined in a small space with no possibility of escape, these conflicts escalate and soon become pure torture, with bloody consequences for both rabbits. This is when you must intervene immediately with castration (see page 85), preferably early on at 10 to 14 weeks of age before the first disputes begin. Then the prospects for continued peaceful coexistence are the best.

Two does: Sometimes they get along well, but when they are in heat, they are inclined to defend their territory against rival females. If you introduce a castrated buck, this usually restores harmony. Sometimes, though, neutering is recommended for does as well (see page 85).

Determining the Sex

Not infrequently, two supposed does surprise their unsuspecting owner "miraculously" with unexpected offspring. This happens more often than you would suspect. That's why I recommend that you have the sex of two young rabbits determined early on, preferably by two experts, for example,

**DID YOU
KNOW THAT . . .**

. . . ear length is an indicator of adult size?

All young rabbits look small and cute. If you have a spacious outdoor enclosure, your pet's future size may not make any difference. Many rabbit lovers even prefer the "cuddly big ones" because they are often calmer and more even tempered than the dwarfs. If you want a dwarf rabbit, though, and are not purchasing it from a breeder or someone who can let you see the parents, then look at the youngster's ear length as a sure indication of future size: The longer the ears, the larger and heavier the animal at maturity. An eight-week-old rabbit with an ear length of $2\frac{3}{4}$ to 3 inches (7–8 cm) will weigh $5\frac{1}{2}$ to 9 pounds (2.5–4 kg) when full grown; with an ear length of 4 inches (10 cm) it will grow up to be a giant rabbit. This doesn't apply to Lop rabbits with long droopy ears.

A small group: If you have enough room, you can also keep two pairs, a female with two castrated bucks, or two castrated males with a doe.

your pet dealer, the breeder, or a veterinarian. If you would like to attempt it yourself, you can try using my description. To check the sex, look at the close-up photo of two eight-week-old dwarf rabbits on page 55.

Bored with Bunny

"Our ten-year-old daughter Melanie has two dwarf rabbits that she took great care of in the beginning. Lately, though, she's interested only in her new computer and totally ignores her two pets. I'm tired of arguing with her about this constantly, and I'm even considering giving the animals away."

Unfortunately, children are not miniature grown-ups. They live more intuitively and spontaneously, but no less seriously. If a child wants a pet and solemnly promises you "on her honor" that she will take care of it forever, then the child means it at the time. Her enthusiasm and her desire to have a little creature like this to love crowd out everything else. True love, however, means something different: having respect for another living creature and its needs, assuming responsibility, and being there for it every day.

Children learn through example

If you give away the two rabbits now because you're tired of arguing with Melanie, what do you think this will teach your daughter? Responsibility and compassion for others? That conflicts can be resolved by talking things over? Or instead that animals are objects that you can just discard when they're no longer fun?

Firm guidelines help

Make a weekly schedule with Melanie. Together, you and she can write down all the chores that have to be done along with fixed times, just like a class schedule. Even though Melanie is already ten years old, she still needs your help. Talk it over with her: What do we want to do together? What can and will you take care of alone? You have to be consistent, check the completed assignments, and in the future avoid criticizing her constantly. Instead, be lavish with your praise and appreciation when Melanie has done a job well. That's a much better way to motivate her!

Make learning fun

Take advantage of your daughter's enthusiasm for her computer. There are lots of Internet forums where children can discuss their rabbits with each other. Ask her teacher if it's possible to cover pets in biology class. The children could all give little oral reports on their pets. Sometimes role-playing teaches children more than words alone. How do rabbits hear? How do they see and smell? Why not pretend to be a rabbit? Or maybe you could play the part of Melanie and let your daughter be a little animal so she can see from this perspective how her pets feel about the way she treats them.

The bottom left photo shows a doe, and the one on the bottom right is a buck.

How to Determine the Sex

To prevent your wriggling rabbit from slipping out of your hands and hurting himself in a fall, it's best to start by placing a thick blanket on the table and then sit down on the edge of the table along with the animal. The correct way to hold a rabbit is like that shown in the photo on page 79 for cleaning the genital area. With one hand, grasp the loose skin on the back of the rabbit's neck (the scruff) and turn him over firmly, belly side up. Support the animal against your chest and immediately grasp him beneath his front legs so he is now immobilized and supported safely in front of you. The rabbit feels the least stressed in this position. Now with the thumb and index finger of your other hand you can gently spread apart the genital and anal areas. The circular anal opening in both sexes is at the base of the tail, and the genital opening is above it, toward the belly. In males the genital opening is also circular. If you press gently on the buck's lower belly, his penis will emerge. In the doe, on the other hand, you can clearly see the slitlike genital opening.

1 **Doe.** This youngster is eight weeks old. You can clearly see the anal opening at the bottom, closest to the tail, and above it the genital opening (slit-shaped vagina).

2 **Buck.** This picture also shows a young animal. You see the anal opening below, and above it the circular genital opening. The small penis protrudes only slightly and thus is difficult to see.

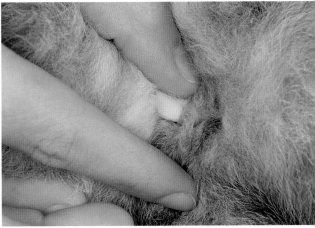

Acclimating Gently

How much time a dwarf needs to acclimate depends on temperament, previous history, and your assistance. A shy animal requires more time and patience than a self-confident one, who before long is hopping around cheerfully in the cage.

To bring your bunny home safely, I recommend the pet carrier shown on page 52. When you purchase one, make sure it has doors in front and on top, as shown in the photo. That makes handling the animals easier. I suggest you get a carrier about 12 inches (30 cm) wide and 16 inches (40 cm) long so that you can even use it later to transport two full-grown dwarfs to the veterinarian.

Quiet, Please!

Once you've arrived home, immediately place your dwarf rabbits in the cage you've prepared for them. Now the new arrivals need some peace and quiet so they can explore their new home. You can sit down quietly nearby and watch them. Are they still crouching terrified in their nest box, or are they already hopping around in their new home? If a dwarf begins to groom himself—rabbits do that only where they feel safe and secure—or starts to eat, then he has gotten over the initial shock.

Tip: Don't make any sudden changes in their diet. In general, rabbits can't tolerate that. If the newcomers were fed only pellets before, for example, you shouldn't start by putting two handfuls of greens in their bowl right away. Instead, proceed slowly, "leaf by leaf," and watch to be sure the rabbits don't react with diarrhea (see Feeding guidelines, page 70).

Guidelines for Getting Along

▶ Always approach a rabbit slowly from the front. Speak to her kindly and let her make contact by sniffing your open hand (sniffing contact).

▶ You will be less intimidating to the little rabbit if you squat down so you're at eye level with the animal. Don't just lean over.

▶ Never grab your rabbit from above (like a bird of prey) without first "introducing" yourself (see photos, pages 58/59).

▶ Make it possible for your rabbits to go in and out of their home on their own. Rabbits like that better than always having their owner put them in and take them out.

▶ Right from the start, feed your rabbits special treats directly from your hand, calling them over and using their names, like this: "Hannibal, come here. Dandelion." This way your pets learn to associate your hand with something good and will gladly let you coax them over.

▶ Never chase after a rabbit, even if he runs away. For one thing, he's usually faster than you, and for another it

Carrot tops are a treat you can use to coax
a rabbit to come to you.

will only cause him to panic (see
page 133).

Lifting and Carrying

Lifting and carrying a dwarf rabbit
correctly is often difficult, especially for
children. If you hesitate rather than
grasp the animal firmly, you can pinch
or squeeze her. This makes her struggle
even harder, she scratches, and before
you know it there's an accident. Your
pet can hurt herself badly by a fall from
this height. Here are several ways to
pick up and carry a rabbit correctly:

Very young rabbits: As long as your
bunny is still small, like the animal in
the photo on page 51, you can clasp
him from the front with both hands so
that he sits safely cradled in your palms
and pick him up.

Basket transport: Lift the dwarf up
quickly and immediately place her in a
basket (see photo, page 59). Snuggled in
the basket with something solid
beneath her paws, your dwarf can now
be picked up together with the basket
and carried. This is much less stressful
for the rabbit.

▶ **1** **Let your rabbit sniff** your open hand to make sure he knows you. Speak to him in a friendly tone of voice.

▶ **2** **Next gently** stroke his back so he gets used to being touched, then pick him up.

▶ **3** **Children usually have** problems picking up a dwarf properly. A basket like the one on page 59 provides a safe way to carry a dwarf rabbit.]

Now you can tuck the basket under your arm or, if it has a sturdy handle, use that to carry it. To be on the safe side, always keep one hand on the animal's back.

Carrying the rabbit on your arm: For rabbits who squirm like crazy, this is the most secure hold: With your right hand, grasp the "scruff," the loose skin on the rabbit's back around the shoulder blades (don't pinch!). With your left hand supporting the rabbit's hindquarters and back legs, pick him up. Don't let the rabbit dangle in midair when you do this, not even for a moment. Carry the rabbit on your bent left arm. Sometimes it calms the rabbit if he can snuggle his head in the crook of your arm. Your right hand remains resting on his neck so you can grab him quickly if he starts to fidget.

The "cat hold": Grasp the dwarf rabbit with one hand from the side below her chest and clasp the animal's front legs (→ photo, page 50). Immediately support the hindquarters with your

other hand, immobilizing the legs between your thumb and middle finger. Put the index finger of this hand between the rabbit's legs so you don't squeeze her too tightly. This hold takes a bit of practice, but many rabbits like it.

Tip: Never lift a rabbit by the ears! That's cruel!

When a New Rabbit Moves In

All rabbits are very territorial and live in a definite social hierarchy. Never imagine, then, that you can simply place a newcomer in a cage where another rabbit has already made territorial claims. If your dwarf has been living alone and now you want to introduce another rabbit as a companion, you need to be patient. After all, you don't make friends with someone right away and then immediately move in with him or her. Whether the two animals get along depends on many factors. As I

explained previously, early neutering and pairing of different sexes helps ensure a peaceful introduction. You should also be careful not to put two dominant rabbits together, because each will want to be boss. Both animals must be healthy and similar in age. Keeping these prerequisites in mind, you can proceed as follows:

Plenty of room on neutral ground: Have the rabbits meet each other for the first time in a place where the resident rabbit has never been and therefore will not immediately defend as his territory. This can be a room in your house unfamiliar to the animal, or you can set up a movable "bonding pen" for the purpose out in the yard. Provide plenty of places to run and hide in the form of houses, tunnels, and boxes, but make sure these haven't already been marked. This bonding pen should be as large as possible, 12 yards^2 (10 m^2) or more: The smaller the space, the greater the stress and resulting aggression. If necessary, open up another area to create additional escape routes. Scatter little treats all around to make the first meeting more "palatable."

TIP

Outdoor rabbits

Don't put your rabbits outside until the veterinarian has vaccinated them against RHD and myxomatosis if possible (see page 87), even though rabbits in the U.S. do not require annual vaccinations. In cold weather dwarf rabbits may go outside only if they have been living in the outdoor enclosure and have a warm winter coat.

MY PET

Where do your rabbits like to hide?

Wild rabbits live in burrows, and dwarf rabbits like to hide, too, whether in a cage, an indoor exercise area, or an outdoor enclosure. Test to find what your dwarf likes best.

The test begins:
- ○ A hollow log
- ○ A wooden house
- ○ A cardboard box in which you cut a variety of entrances to slip through
- ○ A willow tent
- ○ A play tunnel for rabbits

My test results:

Observe: During the initial encounter, stay nearby so you can intervene if the rabbits start to fight. It's completely normal for the animals to chase each other. It's different, though, if the adversaries bite each other seriously and one animal is so intimidated that he retreats in terror and maybe even stops eating. You can find out how to handle these problems in Chapter 8, page 130.

Guinea Pigs and Rabbits

Many pet owners believe they are doing their dwarf rabbit a favor if they get a guinea pig as a companion for her. Yet the two pets differ so much in behavior, body language, and requirements that their coexistence, marked by misunderstandings, is at best a sort of friendship of last resort. Even the frequent observation that "they snuggle together so affectionately" is unfortunately nothing more than human misinterpretation. Both species do indeed live in social groups, but snuggling together and mutual grooming are first and foremost important social behaviors of rabbits. Guinea pigs, in contrast, huddle together more out of insecurity and normally do not groom each other. And how should the rather silent rabbit understand the complex vocal repertoire of the guinea pig?

Furthermore, the smaller defenseless guinea pig is often harassed so badly by a rutting buck or a doe in heat that the guinea pig can be severely injured. To communicate with each other and satisfy their social needs, both rabbits and guinea pigs must have another member of their own species!

Rabbits and Cats

When cats play with other cats, they love to surprise each other by leaping out of hiding places and engaging in wrestling matches. A rabbit, however, doesn't enjoy this at all. Either the rabbit is frightened nearly to death, or else he goes after his supposed enemy, the cat, with tooth and nail and chases kitty up onto a bookcase with a furious biting attack.

In my house, rabbits and cats each live in groups with others of their kind. Encounters between adult animals proceed peacefully because my rabbits are quite self-assured and my house cats are rather placid in temperament. However, when I'm raising both baby cats and baby rabbits at the same time, I keep the young of both species strictly separated in different areas. Even if your cats and rabbits seem to get along peaceably with each other, it's still true that trust is good, but supervision is safer.

Rabbits and Dogs

Even though you can train a dog to obey better than a cat, you should never leave dogs and rabbits alone together without supervision. Rabbits, after all, are among the dog's natural prey, and even a well-trained dog can have a weak moment. If the dog makes one little "snap" or "charge," even if he's just playing and doesn't really mean it, it can cost the rabbit's life.

My cat Pepita grooms the Mini Lop. They grew up together and are fond of each other.

Healthful Food
Keeps Dwarfs Fit

A balanced, varied diet is extremely important for the health
of your dwarf rabbits. And naturally every rabbit home needs
plenty of things to chew.

Fresh Greens and Good Hay

In the wild, rabbits eat a wide variety of grasses, herbs, some fruits, and leaves, and they especially enjoy nibbling the young buds and bark from twigs. You should feed your dwarf rabbits a natural diet, too.

Just like wild rabbits, dwarf rabbits need greens as the first ingredients of a healthful diet. Their special digestive system is made to handle a diet of plants low in nutrient value and high in crude fiber.

A Marvel of Nature

The rabbit's digestive system is designed to get the most out of a meager low-calorie diet. As they watch a rabbit eating, though, most owners certainly have no idea what happens next in the animal's body. Yet it's very important to be aware of this chain of events. Only then will you be in a position to offer your dwarf rabbits healthful, appropriate foods.

The teeth: The rabbit bites and chews off his food with his sharp front incisors. Next, the food is ground thoroughly between the molars and moistened with saliva in his mouth. A rabbit's teeth grow constantly, about a third of an inch (1 cm) per month. This means he has to keep wearing his teeth down by chewing. The best thing for this is if the rabbit eats hay and greens and chews on twigs. Grains, on the other hand, as well as some pellets are

not ground thoroughly enough between the animal's molars, but instead are mashed. The result is insufficient tooth wear leading to serious health problems (see page 81).

The stomach: Because the stomach wall is not very well muscled, food can be moved along through the digestive tract only by stuffing in more food from above. As a grazer with a distensible stomach, the rabbit should and does eat small amounts up to 80 times a day. If, on the other hand, a dwarf gobbles down large quantities of food all at once after lengthy periods between meals, this overloads the stomach and

Even at four weeks of age, these two dwarfs like nibbling on twigs. It's a natural, healthful supplement to mother's milk.

can even result in acute bloat. Make hay available to your dwarf rabbits around the clock so that they can nibble at it constantly and keep their digestion functioning well. There is no substitute for hay, and it should make up about 70 percent of the diet.

The intestinal tract: This consists of the small intestine, large intestine, and cecum. The rabbit's digestive system is extremely sensitive; here nutrients are broken down and transformed until they can be absorbed by the blood. An unusual feature of rabbit anatomy is the large cecum, which occupies almost one-third of the abdominal cavity. In this "fermentation chamber" crude fiber is digested by an ingenious bacterial microflora. At the end of this process, the rabbit eliminates the so-called "cecotropes" and then usually re-ingests them directly from the anus. This way the animal gets essential nutrients and vitamins, especially those of the vitamin-B complex. Sometimes you can find these moist, glistening, grapelike clusters of "vitamin pills" along with the usual dry fecal pellets in the cage litter (see photo, page 66). Nature's marvelous arrangement enables the rabbit to get the most out of his nutrient-poor diet, and because his entire digestive system is geared to this, the dwarf rabbit needs a healthful diet with plenty of crude fiber and a low fat content. This means first and foremost hay, grasses, herbs, fresh vegetables, and twigs.

Hay, a Dietary Staple

I've summarized below for you the reasons why hay is so important for maintaining the health of every dwarf rabbit and must be present in the diet:

▸ A crude fiber content of about 25 percent keeps the digestive system working smoothly (see Stomach, page 63).

▸ Hay balances the fermentation process and ensures an alkaline intestinal pH (pH 8–9). This is important for a healthy intestinal flora. It also prevents dangerous hair balls in the digestive tract (so-called bezoars). Longhair rabbits are especially at risk here since they ingest long loose hairs and swallow them during grooming.

▸ Chewing hay wears down the ever-growing teeth naturally, so the animals develop fewer dental problems.

▸ Hay is not fattening and can be eaten all the time.

▸ It is the ideal diet for rabbits with gastrointestinal problems.

▸ Chewing hay is a healthful recreational activity when things get boring.

Note that alfalfa hay is for very young rabbits. Older rabbits should be fed a grass hay such as timothy or meadow hay. Many rabbit owners use pelleted feed as well as hay.

How do you recognize good hay?

▸ It contains a wide variety of grasses, flowers, and herbs. Commercially available mountain-grass hay should come from a natural meadow, as illustrated on page 65.

Forage Plants

The meadow ▶

Pick fresh dandelion greens (not flowers) and grasses from spring until fall in many lawns and meadows. Avoid fertilizers and pesticides. Feed your dwarfs a wildflower meadow like the one, right.

◀ Medicinal plants

English Plantain (photo far left) and yarrow usually grow along roadsides. Mixed in with your dwarfs' food, fresh or dried, they prevent digestive problems and have an anti-inflammatory effect.

Twigs ▶

Dwarf rabbits are especially fond of twigs from horn-beam and hazelnut trees (photo far right). For a healthful treat, you can let your bunnies chew on twigs with buds, green leaves, or fall foliage.

▶ It has a pleasant aroma.
▶ Good hay is greenish in color, not yellowish or gray.
▶ It should feel rather rough and not too soft (roughage).
▶ Unsuitable: dusty, old, woody, damp, or moldy hay

Hay is essential for your dwarfs' digestion. Make sure it's always available.

Tip: Hay should be freely available around the clock in your rabbit's home. I recommend offering it in a hay rack (see photo, page 75). If you place it on the floor, the animals will get it dirty quickly.

The Right Beverage

Dwarf rabbits always need a freely available supply of fresh, clean drinking water regardless of the weather or method of feeding. Many rabbits drink a lot, others drink little—leave it up to your pets. No rabbit has ever had "a drop too much to drink," but more than one has suffered from thirst because no water was available! Whether you provide it in a gravity water bottle with sipper tube or in a stoneware bowl (see page 70), water is best served cool, but not ice cold. Boil heavily chlorinated tap water first and then let it cool. If the nitrate concentration in your tap water is high, give your pets noncarbonated mineral water.

Tip: Rabbits can't tolerate milk! Use chamomile tea for therapeutic purposes only.

Greens Are Tops

Beginning in spring, I gradually switch from feeding my rabbits fresh foods (vegetables and greens) to giving them all the wonderful grasses, herbs, and flowers Mother Nature has to offer. All wild rabbits feed primarily on these plants, so this is the closest thing to a natural diet for your pets.

Tip: If your dwarf rabbits are not accustomed to this fare, then get them used to it gradually, "leaf by leaf," over a period of three to four weeks. Don't make any sudden radical changes in their diet! And never assume your rabbits can recognize poisonous plants.

Recommended collecting sites:

▶ all-natural meadows, especially in nature preserves, organic farms, and parks if these are set up as "biotopes."

Dry fecal pellets and, in contrast, the grapelike clusters of cecotropes.

▼

FRESH VEGETABLES AND HERBS FROM KITCHEN AND GARDEN

SUITABLE AND UNSUITABLE FRESH FOODS

Especially recommended	**Vegetables with Greens:** carrots, fennel, celeriac, celery, Jerusalem artichoke, turnip dark, leafy lettuces (only in summer, unsprayed, from the garden!) broccoli (leaves and tops) **Herbs and medicinal plants:** basil, borage, watercress, dill, chamomile, chervil, lovage, lemon balm, oregano, parsley, yarrow
Recommended	**Vegetables/Tubers:** squash, parsnip, chicory, zucchini, parsley root **Only leaves of** corn, peas, beans, soybeans
Feed only in small amounts; test for digestibility	dark, leafy lettuces (in winter from the greenhouse); corn salad (lamb's lettuce) is also easily digested Chinese, red, and green cabbage varieties (healthful, but cause gas); Chinese cabbage and kohlrabi leaves are most easily digested cucumbers (without peel!), Swiss chard, peppers (without stems!) radish greens (very spicy), beet tops, red tomatoes, asparagus, corn kernels (a favorite, but very high in calories)
Not suitable— never feed these!	eggplant, avocado, legumes (peas, lentils), radishes (root), soybeans (the beans), leeks, ornamental gourds, onions, rhubarb; spinach
Warning! Poisonous!	raw potatoes and potato leaves, green tomatoes, tomato leaves, raw beans

PARENTS' EXTRA

Sharing Is Not Always Good

"My two children love sweets more than anything, and they always give their two dwarf rabbits a little. Chocolate cookies are the bunnies' favorite. Are sweets really harmful for their rabbits?"

Rabbits cannot tolerate sweets at all! They cause stomachaches and digestive problems. Discuss this with your children. I'm sure they don't want to hurt their rabbits. The underlying problem is often simple ignorance along with the belief that what we humans enjoy also tastes good to our four-legged friends. And unfortunately, many rabbits have a real sweet tooth: They love to nibble on cookies, chocolates, and even candy.

Healthful snacks for dwarfs

If your children would like to give their rabbits an occasional treat, then please make sure they're healthful ones from now on. Explain to your children which treats are good for the animals. I recommended a piece of apple or a bit of carrot, for example. On page 71 you'll also find a short list of nonperishable treats that you can buy in the pet store. Naturally, these goodies don't replace the rabbits' staple diet of hay, fresh greens, and vegetables.

Learn together and have fun

Take a trip to the countryside with your family and gather healthful plants for your dwarf rabbits to eat. In case you're not much of a botanist, stick a field guide to wildflowers and trees in your pocket (see photos, page 65). You'll find that an outing like this is not only educational, but lots of fun as well (see Recommended Collecting Sites, page 66). Show your children the individual plants either in the wild or as an illustration in the book. Then you're ready to go exploring together. See who's the first to find yarrow, plantain, coltsfoot, bindweed, or a hazelnut tree. But while you're having fun collecting plants, please remember: A dwarf gets only a handful of greens a day, so don't collect too much. Fresh foods should always be crisp; don't let them lie around for days until they wilt. In case your dwarf rabbits aren't familiar with fresh foods yet, you'll have to get them used to this new diet slowly (see Important Feeding Guidelines, page 70).

▸ overgrown plots of land, fallow fields, forest edges
▸ your own organic garden

Don't collect in these places:

▸ along the side of heavily traveled roads (polluted by auto exhaust)
▸ wherever dogs run loose (transmission of disease by droppings)
▸ wherever herbicides and pesticides are used, whether in the garden or in agricultural areas
▸ wherever wild rabbits live (risk of myxomatosis)

Recommended Plants

Wild plants: bindweed, common plantain, strawberry leaves, daisy, grass, dandelion greens (see photos, page 65), coltsfoot, orache, English plantain (see photo, page 65), chickweed, and vetch
Flowers: sunflowers, only the leaves of the plant and the flowers (see photo below); calendula (flowers, stems, and leaves)

Special medicinal herbs: chamomile, lemon balm, sage, yarrow (see photo, page 65)
Kitchen herbs: basil, dill, chervil, oregano, parsley, lovage
Tip: Dwarfs like to eat clover, but it should be mixed in with their food only in small amounts since too much of it causes gas. White clover and alfalfa are tolerated very well. You shouldn't feed your dwarf rabbits red clover.

Fruits and Berries

A piece of apple is especially good as an occasional treat, as is a strawberry or a slice of pear. Apples are even supposed to promote digestion and prevent intestinal problems. Fruits and berries should be fed in very limited quantities (no more than 2 tablespoons a day for 5-pound [2.2 kg] rabbit!), if at all. I advise against all exotic fruits. Many rabbits do indeed like sweet bananas and honeydew melons, but in my opinion even these are not natural foods for rabbits.

Rabbits love to eat sunflower leaves, and these two youngsters are getting some exercise as they stretch to reach them.

Something to Chew On

Regularly feed them twigs with buds and leaves. This helps prevent boredom, wears down their teeth, and provides healthful roughage. In the fall my rabbits also enjoy eating dry leaves.

Highly recommended: hazelnut, hornbeam (see photos, page 65), apple and pear trees

Tolerated only in small amounts: maple, birch, alder, linden, poplar, willow, as well as all fir and spruce twigs. However, willow bark contains salicylic acid compounds similar to aspirin and may create or exacerbate illness.

Not tolerated: all twigs from stone fruit varieties as well as oak and chestnut

Poisonous: yew and arborvitae

The "Rabbit Meadow"

Offer your dwarfs a little meadow of fresh greens to nibble on in winter.

You need: container (10 inches [25 cm] diameter, 4 inches [10 cm] deep), expanded clay pebbles (¼ to ½ inch [5–10 mm]), seed-starting mix, and seeds (e.g., wheat, alfalfa, chervil, or a seed mixture sold as "rabbit meadow")

This is how you do it: Soak about 4 tablespoons of seeds in lukewarm water for four hours. Put about an inch (3 cm) of expanded clay pebbles in the container as a drainage layer. Over this add about 2 inches (5 cm) of seed-starting mix and spread the seeds on the surface. Cover the seeds with ¾ inch (2 cm) of mix, press it down lightly, and water it. Put the container in a window that gets plenty of daylight and keep the soil moist. In two to four weeks, depending on the type of plants, you'll have a tasty "meadow."

Important Feeding Guidelines

▶ Rabbits always need plenty of hay and fresh drinking water.
▶ Always feed your rabbits greens and vegetables that are fresh and clean. If greens are wet from the rain, spin them dry in a hand towel before feeding them to your rabbits. Wash vegetables and fruit well, then dry them off.
▶ Feed your dwarfs regularly, preferably in the morning and evening.
▶ Remove fresh foods from the cage the following morning at the latest.
▶ Don't give them any foods that are frozen, spoiled, moldy, or contaminated with pollutants.

Tip: Never make abrupt changes in diet. Change the diet over a three- to four-week period, exchanging portion for portion.

To prevent food and water bowls from being contaminated with bedding, place them on an aircrete block (2¼ inches [7 cm] high). The block is impregnated with a washable nontoxic dye.

Commercial Pelleted Diets

You can buy pelleted feed in pretty packages. It's always available, keeps for a long time, and is very practical. But are pellets really as healthful as they're claimed to be? Are they advisable for rabbits?

Most pet owners and breeders feed their bunnies pellets. And although the industry is always putting new pelleted diets on the market, rabbit experts and owners are having heated discussions over which pellets should be recommended, or whether it wouldn't be better to eliminate them entirely.

Healthful Pellets

If you don't want to eliminate pelleted feeds, then you should keep the following in mind: Healthful pellets consist primarily of dried vegetables, herbs, and grasses; they have a crude fiber content of at least 16 percent, a maximum fat content of 2 to 3 percent, and a maximum protein content of 15 percent.

Ingredients: Take a close look at the ingredients listed on the label of the pellet package. Don't be misled by colorful packaging and flowery promises. Green and red nuggets in the food are not always vegetables: Sometimes they're just colored bakery products. If the pellet composition is given, the ingredients are always listed in order of abundance from highest to lowest. For instance, if grains are listed first, they make up the greatest percentage of the mixture.

Vitamins: Almost all pellet varieties have added vitamins. It's my opinion that a rabbit given a healthful diet does not need these supplements. If you think vitamin supplements are important, though, you should at least check the expiration date.

Tip: Rabbits like to eat grains, corn, nuts, sugar, and molasses, but they contain far too many calories and lead to digestive and dental problems. Besides, an animal quickly feels full from eating this rich fare and then eats little or no hay, even though it's very important for his digestion.

As explained earlier, the rabbit is by nature a plant eater and not a grain eater.

TIP

Pleasure without remorse

If you would like to offer your rabbit healthful snacks occasionally, I've found these for you in the pet store: pure herb mixtures, green oats, dandelion greens, rose hips, carrot chips, and apple slices (dried, untreated, and above all with no additional ingredients).

◄ *Working for treats prevents boredom. String*
them on a piece of twine and hang them up.

Pellet mixes: In pellet mixes, the animals pick out the fattening bits first and leave behind the healthful green pellets. Pure pelleted feed prevents the rabbits from "fishing out" the choice morsels, but here too you should pay attention to the ingredients. It's best if you don't give your rabbits a pellets-only diet; instead, feed them in small quantities as a supplement.

How much to feed: Give your dwarf about 1 ounce (30 g) of pellets per day as a supplement to hay, greens, and fresh fruits and vegetables. Under no circumstances should you use pellets as a substitute for fresh foods.

Treat Sticks & Co.

Most treat sticks are pure calorie bombs that will make your rabbits fat and upset their sensitive digestive systems. So you're not doing your dwarf rabbits a favor if you spoil them like this. If your rabbits have a healthful diet, they don't need salt licks or mineral stones, either. On the contrary, if they ingest too much of these, they'll get sick.

Tip: Don't feed your rabbits sweets like cookies, chocolate, or cake (see Parents' Extra, page 68); avoid pretzel sticks and table scraps, too.

MY PET

Are your dwarf rabbits little gourmets?

All my rabbits are little gourmets, and they let me know quite plainly which foods they like best. Why not test your pets yourself. What are your dwarf rabbits' favorite foods?

The test begins:
- ○ Ordinary hay or herbal hay?
- ○ All the grass (the entire blade) or just the tender tips?
- ○ A lettuce leaf from the supermarket or one fresh from the garden?
- ○ A twig with tender buds or just the twig?
- ○ A bunch of fresh herbs or dried herbs?

My test results:

Questions on
Nutrition

My dwarf hates hay. What's the reason for this?

Maybe your rabbit just isn't hungry. This happens especially when rabbits are fed generously with pellets, but also if they are given fresh foods for their first meal of the day. Postpone the morning feeding for three to four hours; instead, fill your rabbit's food bowl with tasty herbal hay in the morning. Then watch your hay-hating rabbit turn into a "hay freak."

My three dwarfs live in a permanent outdoor enclosure all year long. What can I do to keep their drinking water from freezing in the winter?

Either place their water bowl in the shelter or fill the bowl several times a day with warm water—it won't freeze so quickly. A friend of mine hung her rabbits' water bottle outside the cage and put a Styrofoam bottle cover over it. You can buy Styrofoam covers for keeping baby bottles warm.

We just got a pair of very young rabbits. Now the seller tells us that the youngsters should eat only a special baby bunny diet and absolutely no greens or fresh fruits and vegetables; otherwise they'll get sick. Is that true?

Yes and no. Under no circumstance should you change your new arrivals' diet right away if they're not accustomed to this food. This is true of all rabbits, though, regardless of how old they are. Continue using the baby bunny diet over the next four weeks and supplement it carefully with small, easily digestible morsels. Start by feeding each dwarf one slice of apple or two parsley leaves or half a carrot (cut lengthwise) or a small piece of fennel daily. Then every day offer a little more fresh food. And don't forget: Hay is the most important food and must always be available. My rabbit babies grow up eating greens and fresh fruits and vegetables along with hay right from the start. They tolerate all these foods very well and thrive splendidly without getting diarrhea or intestinal gas from the fresh foods.

My dwarfs are often allowed to run around outside in the yard, since it is rabbit-proofed. Can rabbits really recognize poisonous plants?

Maybe the instinct is present in wild rabbits, but under no circumstance would I run the risk with our house rabbits. Either limit the exercise area or remove any plants that might be poisonous.

Is it true that rabbits can't tolerate wet grass?

If they are hopping around outside in the rain and nibbling on the lawn, that won't harm them. However, if I feed them fresh-cut grass that's wet with rain, I always dry it first in a hand towel and then let it finish drying on a linen towel. I have found that this agrees with my rabbits better. Besides, my animals won't even touch grass and dandelions if they're really wet.

The veterinarian thinks my dwarf is overweight. Can you give me tips for a diet?

Overweight rabbits aren't just less attractive; they also die sooner than slimmer rabbits. As far as unhealthful preferences are concerned, there are practically no differences between humans and animals. Rabbits love sweets and fatty foods, too. Give this diet a try. Eliminate fattening things like treat sticks and pellets high in grains from the menu. One day a week feed only hay and water. Under no circumstance, however, should you let your rabbits go hungry. Prescribe regular out-of-cage time and lots of exercise for your little butterball. Hide twigs, greens, and other healthful treats in the exercise pen, or hang them up so your rabbit has to stretch to reach them. Dwarf rabbits kept alone often lie around lazily out of boredom. A companion rabbit sometimes works wonders in this case. Of course, the introduction must be handled very carefully (see page 58).

How much should a full-grown dwarf weigh, actually?

If your rabbit is a purebred dwarf, she should weigh between 2 and 3⅓ pounds (1.0–1.5 kg). Mini Lops weigh up to 4½ pounds (2.0 kg). All mixed-breed dwarfs can—but don't have to— weigh more. Carefully run your hands over your dwarf rabbit's body. If she has little rolls of fat and you can no longer feel her ribs, then your dwarf is definitely overweight.

Our dwarf rabbits eat their own droppings, although they get enough to eat. Why do they do that?

There's no reason to feel disgusted. The rabbits are not eating normal feces, but rather the so-called cecotropes. These are soft, moist, and look like a cluster of grapes (see photo, page 66). Sometimes you can find them in the cage litter, but normally the dwarf rabbit ingests them directly from the anus. Cecotropes contain essential vitamins and crude protein.

Hygiene and Health Care

A clean home and proper care are the best way to keep your rabbit healthy. If he gets sick, though, you should take him to a veterinarian right away.

Proper Care Prevents Disease

Good hygiene is essential for keeping rabbits. Regularly cleaning cages, cage furnishings, and exercise pens is just as important for your dwarf rabbits as carefully monitoring their health.

In order for the fastidious rabbit to feel happy and healthy, he needs a clean, well-kept home and exercise area. Damp, dirty bedding not only smells unpleasant, but is also a breeding ground for all sorts of bacteria and encourages the spread of disease.

Cleanliness Is Compulsory

How often you need to clean the rabbit cage and exercise area depends on several factors, including how many animals you keep and how much time they spend there. I pay a lot of attention to cleanliness at my house, because decades of experience with raising and keeping a variety of animals has taught me that good hygiene is an extremely important aspect of health care. By this I don't mean the unbridled use of cleaning products and disinfectants, but rather regular cleaning of the animals' home along with its contents.
Daily: Scrub all food and water bowls under hot water, rinse them off, and then dry them well. Scrub water bottles with a bottle brush and clean the metal drinking tube with a cotton swab. Wherever the straw has been trampled down, loosen it up with your hands so

that the fecal pellets drop down into the litter. Remove all soiled litter in the toilet areas and replace it with fresh. Thoroughly vacuum the carpet and straw mats in the indoor exercise pens. I use an industrial vacuum cleaner (available in home improvement centers) for this purpose because it has better suction as well as a larger capacity and doesn't get clogged right away if bits of straw are vacuumed up. If you keep your rabbits on the balcony or in an outdoor enclosure, you should remove the fecal pellets there every day as well (see Danger! Maggots! page 91).
Weekly: Replace all the litter and

Rabbits groom each other and so reinforce their friendship.

bedding in the housing, litter boxes and digging boxes with fresh. Scrub everything, including houses, perches, and fixtures, under hot water and then dry them.

Tip: Urine crystals, which sometimes collect in the bottom tray of the cage, can be removed as follows: Fill the tray an inch or so (a few cm) deep with warm water, dissolve two to three tablespoons of citric acid in it (available at the drugstore), and let it work for half an hour. Then dump everything out, rinse with clean water—and you're finished.

If you have several rabbits: In this

A Well-groomed Coat

Rabbits groom themselves thoroughly. Nevertheless, our regular assistance with coat care helps keep them healthy. Hair balls can form, especially when the animal is shedding and swallows too much fur as she licks her coat; in the worst case, this can lead to gastrointestinal obstruction. Rabbits that are kept outside all year-round adjust their coat to the weather conditions. In spring they lose their dense, warm winter fur and wear the lighter summer coat until early fall. Then they change again. Shedding is

Dwarf rabbits are very clean animals. They clean their fur thoroughly **several times a day** using their forepaws and tongues.

case, I suggest you make arrangements with a neighboring farmer. I buy fresh straw from "my" farmer, and in exchange he lets me dump my old litter on his manure heap free of charge. This is a major advantage, because disposing of the quantities of litter required by several rabbits would be quite a problem otherwise. For transporting and storing the litter I use leaf bags made of tear-proof synthetic material with a capacity of 30 gallons (120 L) and 68 gallons (260 L) (from the garden center). These bags have convenient handles and don't fall over constantly when you're filling them.

less intense in house rabbits, but instead goes on continuously over a longer period.

Tip: If your dwarfs live in an outdoor pen year-round, you should never bring them into your heated house "to warm up" in winter when it's especially cold outside. Conversely, you should never let a house rabbit go outside in the snow and cold for a "breath of fresh air." I'm always getting questions from readers on this subject. An abrupt temperature change like this poses a real threat to your rabbit's health! You would never think of running around in the snow dressed just in a T-shirt and sandals, nor would you sit in your heated house wearing heavy winter clothing (see page 42).

1 **Wipe the ear** with a clean tissue. Don't use cotton swabs: You could injure the dwarf rabbit's ear canal with them.

Check the teeth to make sure **2** they are wearing down naturally and are properly aligned. The upper incisors must close just over the lower ones (scissors bite).

3 **The genital area** sometimes gets caked with secretions. Remove these regularly with a cotton swab soaked in baby oil. It works best if you support your rabbit and hold him like this.

The toenails grow continuously, **4** and if they are not worn down sufficiently, they must be trimmed with a nail clipper. Have a veterinarian or rabbit expert show you how to do this the first time.

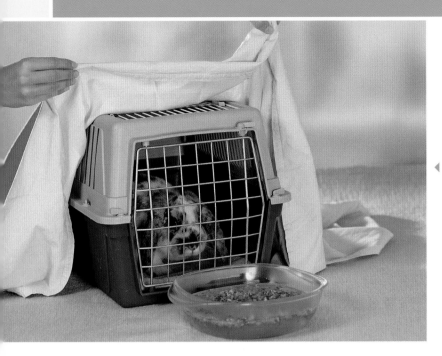

◄ *This helps for respiratory ailments: Pour boiling water over chamomile flowers (from the pharmacy only). Put the rabbit in the carrier and cover everything with a lightweight cloth. Allow the rabbit to inhale the vapors for about 15 minutes.*

Rabbits with normal-length fur: Once a month, and once to twice a week when your rabbit is shedding, brush her coat in the direction of growth using a natural-bristle brush. Afterward remove any loose hair with a damp leather cloth.

Longhair rabbits: Their coat tends to become matted and, depending on length and hair structure, must be groomed every day. The best thing for you to use are the special combs and brushes made for grooming longhair cats. Rabbits with soft angora wool usually require even more coat care. These animals must be sheared completely. That's why you should give plenty of thought to whether you really want to put this much effort into grooming your rabbits (see Tip, page 25).

Tip: Never give a rabbit a shower or bath! If necessary, you can carefully trim away any fur in the anal region that's matted with feces. Soften up residual clumps in a chamomile bath and then dry the animal well (see Danger! Maggots! page 91).

Additional Grooming Tasks

Ear care: The best way to remove excess wax from the ears is with a clean tissue (see photo, page 79). Lop rabbits in particular need to have their long droopy ears checked regularly. Never use cotton swabs for cleaning, because they can injure your dwarf's ear canal. If there are signs of waxy buildup, crustiness, ear shaking, or itching, take the animal to the veterinarian immediately!

Cleaning the genital area: In the hairless skin folds on either side of the genital opening there are inguinal glands that produce pheromones (scents) (see page 19). They give off a heavy, sweetish aroma. Deposits of secretions often accumulate there, and you should remove them regularly with a cotton swab soaked in baby oil. Cleaning the genital area helps prevent inflammation (see photo, page 79). Examining the teeth: Place the dwarf on a nonskid pad on the table. Grasp him beneath his chest with your left hand and hold his front paws between your thumb and middle finger (see photo, page 79). Now use the thumb of your left hand to pull his lower lip down slightly, being careful not to press on his larynx. With the fingers of your right hand, pull back his upper lip a bit until the incisors are visible. In normally aligned teeth, the incisors of the upper jaw close just over the teeth of the lower jaw like a pair of scissors (scissors bite). When the rabbit gnaws or chews, the continuously growing teeth rub against each other and are worn down. For healthy tooth wear, it's important to give your rabbit a natural diet with hay, greens, and fresh fruits and vegetables as well as twigs to nibble. **Tip:** This natural abrasion is no longer possible in rabbits with "trap teeth" or with a more severe genetic (hereditary) misalignment of the teeth ("malocclusion") caused by a shortening of the upper jaw. Here the incisors of the upper jaw bend inward and those of the lower jaw grow forward out of the mouth (so-called "buck teeth" or "wolf teeth"). Once they reach a certain length, the dwarf rabbit is no longer able to eat, and his teeth must be trimmed regularly by the veterinarian. Without special training, it's very difficult to check the molars farther back in the mouth. However, if you notice that the fur around your rabbit's mouth is caked with saliva and the animal chews when her mouth is empty, you must take her to the veterinarian right away. The reason for this is that sharp edges or spurs form on the molars and can then penetrate the mucous membranes of the tongue and inside of the mouth, causing severe inflammation.

Toenail care: The toenails grow constantly and often are not worn down enough, especially in house rabbits. I check my dwarfs' toenails every two months (see Tip, below). If they get too long, they can bend inward and dig into the paws. I've already seen a few of these sad cases in animal shelters. These poor animals could no longer walk, or managed to do so only with great pain. Toenails have to be trimmed before they get too long. The rabbit has five toenails on each front paw and four on each hind paw. A toenail of normal length is a bit longer than the fur on the paw, and the tip is visible when the rabbit is standing. It is not turned backward. If you have never trimmed your rabbit's toenails, you should first have a veterinarian or an expert show you how it's done.

TIP

Wearing down those toenails

Indoor and balcony housing: Place a natural stone slab in the digging box underneath the sand mixture. Outdoor enclosure: Use a variety of substrates, including sand, soil, rock, and bark mulch. Provide a layer of soil (see page 46) or, if this is not possible, make a dirt mound for them to dig in.

How to trim toenails: You can use a guillotine-type nail trimmer (available in pet stores) or a fingernail clipper to cut your rabbit's toenails. Trim them about ¼ inch (7 mm) beyond the blood vessels (the living part) (see photo, page 79). In colorless toenails, the so-called "quick" is visible as a reddish area. To see where the blood vessels are in darker toenails, shine a bright flashlight through the nail from below. If you injure the blood vessels despite all your precautions, press a clean handkerchief on the injury, then disinfect and protect the spot with a spray bandage.

Regular exercise in the fresh air keeps the rabbit's cardiovascular system in shape and strengthens her immunity. Extreme temperature changes, on the other hand, are harmful.

When Your Dwarf Rabbit Is Sick

Rabbits are naturally quite hardy. Errors in husbandry such as improper diet, lack of exercise, stress, or poor hygiene are frequently to blame when a dwarf rabbit gets sick.

If you watch your rabbits closely every day, you'll be quick to notice any changes. The sooner you recognize signs of disease, the greater the chances for recovery (see Table, page 51).

Be Observant!

Wild rabbits are prey animals, and they rely on escape to survive (and are thus called flight animals). It is in their nature to keep still and retreat to a safe place when they are sick or injured. This way they don't attract attention and can often avoid speedy capture by some predator. Our dwarf rabbits behave the same way. A dog with an injured paw would come limping up to his mistress or master, stretch out his paw with a whimper, and expect words of comfort and first aid. The dwarf, on the other hand, sits quietly in the corner of his cage, even with a broken leg, and tries to be as inconspicuous as possible. Time and again I hear about rabbits like this whose owners weren't observant enough and didn't notice anything unusual; the animals were taken to the veterinarian too late or not at all and died well before their time.

First Signs of Disease

Improper diet, dirty living conditions, too little exercise, too few activities, and stress all weaken the rabbit's immune system. As a result, he can get sick. Watch for changes in behavior and check each and every one of your rabbits regularly.

Behavior: Is the dwarf hopping around as usual and showing an interest in her surroundings? Sick rabbits prefer to withdraw and crouch apathetically in their house or in a corner.

Appetite: Does the animal approach you as usual, and is his appetite good?

TIP

Hold tight!

Rabbits are silent patients, but by no means are they always quiet and cooperative if you want to treat them. For your own safety, it's important to restrain the animal well. If you have problems with the recommended holds, have your veterinarian demonstrate them for you first.

Rabbits must not fast. The daily hay ration is the basic prerequisite for a properly functioning digestive system (see page 63).

Body: Run your hands over each of your animals at least once a day. Stroke the fur and feel all over the body, including the belly and the legs. Check the anal area to be sure it is clean and dry.

Feces: When you clean the enclosure and cage, always take a look at the fecal pellets. Are the little balls dry and well formed (see photo, page 66)? Soft, mushy stools indicate diarrhea.

The Right Veterinarian

Even though I've given you a few suggestions in this handbook for treating health problems, they are in no way a substitute for a visit to the veterinarian. Quite a few diseases have similar symptoms in the early stages. They begin as harmless ailments and can quickly become acute and life threatening. It's very difficult for a layperson to make the correct assessment all the time. Rather than

hesitating, take your sick dwarf to the veterinarian early on. To make sure your rabbit receives the best possible treatment, pay close attention to the following:

The small-animal specialist: Not every veterinarian who knows a lot about dogs and cats is also a competent rabbit specialist. Ask about this specifically first and check with other rabbit owners.

A thorough examination: A good veterinarian does not make hasty diagnoses. He questions you first in detail about your sick rabbit and gives the bunny a thorough general examination.

Good advice: Ask the veterinarian to explain the treatments and medications to you and discuss additional measures in detail. Show that you're interested, and ask questions if you don't understand something. That's quite within your rights. If you want to learn something, though, you have to be able to listen and not act like you know it all. A good veterinarian is also aware of his limitations. When necessary, he will refer you to a specialist or a clinic. If you still have doubts and are not satisfied with the care your pet is receiving, don't hesitate to consult another expert. But if you are satisfied and your dwarf is being well treated, the veterinarian will appreciate a word of praise.

Alternative treatment methods: Antibiotics are sometimes unavoidable, but they're not necessary for every little thing. The rabbit's digestive system can be especially sensitive to these drugs. Ask about alternative therapies (natural remedies, homeopathy).

TIP

Important information for the veterinarian

To help the veterinarian with his diagnosis, you should note down the following in advance: Age and sex of the dwarf. Which symptoms did you notice and when? Has the rabbit been eating and drinking? Bring along the vaccination certificate if you have it. If your rabbit has diarrhea, bring a fecal sample.

A warm summer shower doesn't bother a healthy rabbit.

Is Neutering or Sterilization Advisable?

Both neutering and sterilization are tried-and-true methods of birth control. Since the concepts are still frequently confused, here's an explanation of the differences.

Neutering: In this case the sex organs are removed. Removal of the testicles in bucks is called castration, and removal of the ovaries and uterus in does is known as spaying.

Sterilization: In this operation the spermatic cords are severed in the buck, and the oviducts in the doe. The reproductive organs are thus retained. Sterilization is neither customary nor recommended in practice, since with this method the sex hormones continue to be produced and all the associated behavioral and health problems persist. But why should rabbits be neutered? Rabbits are social animals. Keeping just one rabbit is not natural for this species. Neutering helps rabbits live together more peaceably, makes them generally easier to keep as pets, and prevents health problems. Neutered rabbits

▸ get along better with other rabbits;
▸ no longer have offspring;
▸ are easier to litter-box train;
▸ spray and mark less;
▸ are more even tempered in their overall behavior, including in their relationships with humans;
▸ have healthier and longer lives.

The right time

In principle, it is best to neuter rabbits when they are young. If you have an unneutered adult, discuss the risks and benefits of the neuter surgery with your veterinarian.

Buck: Castration is performed as soon as the testicles descend into the scrotum, which is to say with the onset of sexual maturity (three to four months of age); early castration at 10 to 14 weeks is also possible.

Doe: She has an estrus cycle and is designed by nature to be very fertile. If pet does are not spayed, this increases their risk of developing mammary, uterine, and ovarian cancer during their lifetime. Scientific studies have verified this, and I can only confirm it based on firsthand knowledge of many cases. Spaying is especially recommended for does who repeatedly undergo false pregnancy and are always in heat.

Tip: Take your doe only to an experienced veterinarian or to a small-animal clinic with proven success in neutering female animals.

Things to keep in mind with neutering

Before surgery: In contrast to other pets (dogs, cats), rabbits should not fast before surgery. For one thing, a rabbit cannot vomit and consequently cannot aspirate his vomit. For another, a rabbit should not fast because this puts stress on the sensitive digestive system. Give your bunny hay and light fare (apple, carrot, fennel) in the evening and morning before the scheduled surgery.

Postoperative care at home: To promote wound healing in the first three to four days after neutering, place the rabbit on towels or paper in the cage rather than on straw. If bucks and does live together, a buck can go back in the pen with the does immediately after surgery only if he was castrated early (at 10 to 14 weeks). A male rabbit who has already mated or who was castrated after the onset of sexual maturity must be housed separately from the does after castration. Male rabbits have been documented to be able to store sperm for up to 60 days. Therefore, a castrated male can still impregnate an intact (not spayed) female during that time. Males should be separated from intact does

> For many diseases, **natural remedies** promote the healing process.

Natural remedies aid the healing process and frequently have fewer side effects.

for 60 days postoperatively. Otherwise, there is the danger that any sperm still present may impregnate the female. Many animals suffer from low body temperature after surgery. Normal body temperature is 101 to 104°F (38.5–40°C). You can tell if the body temperature is below normal even without measuring it by feeling the ears. If they are very cold, you must warm the animal up right away. The best way to do this is by placing an infrared lamp on the roof of the cage. The chilled animal can then sit under it as needed. The dwarf rabbit should begin eating again the day after surgery at the latest. If she doesn't, you must take her to the veterinarian. A few weeks ago I had a little patient who wouldn't eat after surgery. After consulting with my veterinarian, we force-fed Munchkin for two days with a semi-solid food (see Critical Care). That helped. Soon the youngster started eating again and is now perfectly healthy.

Vaccinations Save Lives

Vaccinations to protect our rabbits against three life-threatening diseases are available in some countries. In principle, every healthy rabbit can be vaccinated after a certain minimum age. Ask your veterinarian for details.

RHD (Rabbit Hemorrhagic Disease)

This highly contagious and fatal viral disease, which originated in China, has spread like a plague over all of Europe. For this reason it is sometimes known as Chinese Plague.

CHECKLIST

Your Rabbit's Medicine Chest

Natural remedies, available in the pharmacy:

○ **Rescue Remedy (Bach Flowers):** first aid for accidents, shock

○ **Traumeel (tablets):** for injuries, inflammation

○ **Nux Vomica 6D (globules):** regulates mild digestive disorders

○ **Euphrasia eyedrops:** for reddened, irritated eyes

○ **Arnica 30C (globules):** promotes wound healing, good after surgery, fractures, bite wounds

○ **Swedish bitters:** heals and disinfects minor wounds

○ **Chamomile/Thyme:** for inhalation, has an expectorant and anti-inflammatory effect on respiratory organs

Available only from the veterinarian:

○ **Critical Care:** assisted-feeding formula

Available from pet product suppliers:

○ **Bird Bene-Bac** (consists of live, freeze-dried bacterial cultures): excellent remedy for restoring balance of intestinal flora or a lactobacillus source that does not have added sucrose (sugar)

Saying Good-bye

"Our dwarf rabbit Maya has a malignant inoperable tumor. She has stopped eating and is in considerable pain. The veterinarian advises us to have her put to sleep. How I should explain this to my six-year-old son, Michael?"

It always hurts when we have to say good-bye to a beloved friend, whether human or animal. In our modern "forever young" society, topics such as growing old, sickness, and death are all too willingly suppressed. As a result, many parents have difficulty explaining death to their children, whether because of their own helplessness, a desire to protect the children, or mere indifference. They'd rather not talk about it and just get back to the business of the day as quickly as possible. Or else they decide to get a replacement animal right away to console their children. But is this the consolation our children need? Wouldn't they far rather have us take their feelings seriously and be there for them? Feeling sad, suffering a loss, and saying good-bye are as much a part of life as joy and happiness.

Talk to them beforehand

Take your son in your arms and explain to him that his little friend is suffering so much and is so sick that prolonging her life would be torture. Tell him that Maya will just fall asleep peacefully in your arms at the veterinarian's and then go to rabbit heaven, where she'll be happy with all the other animals. There's a wonderful story about the rainbow bridge, familiar to many pet owners, that is very comforting. You can read this to your son, too. I think it's beautiful, and you can find it on many animal welfare sites on the Internet.

Rituals help

I don't recommend taking the easy way out and getting rid of your dead pet by taking her to a facility for the disposal of animal bodies. Instead, you and your son should bury your four-legged friend together. A ritual like this helps you deal with your grief and begin the healing process. You can bury Maya in your own yard or have her remains cremated in a pet crematorium and the ashes sent back to you in a small urn. What's important here are the farewell ritual and a memorial spot. My two children made a little cross and the three of us planted flowers on the grave. We said a prayer and lighted a candle. My children still remember this, even today, and I'm glad we shared this moving experience.

Symptoms: Apathy, labored breathing, fever, bleeding from the nose, death accompanied by asphyxiation and convulsions. Sometimes the disease progresses so rapidly that the animal dies before any symptoms appear.

Cause: A calicivirus. It's transmitted from animal to animal by saliva, feces, urine, or blood-sucking insects such as mosquitoes as well as by contaminated objects such as food, bedding, and clothing.

Treatment: The disease is incurable in unvaccinated dwarf rabbits. Vaccination is possible starting at eight weeks of age. Basic immunization (two vaccinations), then an annual booster shot.

Myxomatosis

This disease is also known as "big head disease." It comes from South America and rages like a plague through the wild rabbit population.

Symptoms: The eyelids swell, leading to blindness; severe swelling of the head and genitalia.

Cause: The myxomatosis virus is a member of the poxvirus family. Transmission usually occurs through blood-sucking insects (fleas, mosquitoes), but can it also be transmitted like RHD (see Text, left).

Treatment: In unvaccinated animals, the mortality rate is around 80 percent. To obtain basic immunity, the rabbit must be vaccinated twice, preferably in spring before the mosquito season. After that a booster shot every six months.

Tip: Only rabbits and hares can be infected with myxomatosis and RHD. The disease cannot be transmitted to other animals or people! Especially at risk are all house rabbits living near wild rabbit populations as well as rabbits that come in contact with other infected rabbits or their owners. Since you can never entirely rule out the possibility of infection, both vaccinations are recommended, even for rabbits kept exclusively indoors.

As first aid for heatstroke, place a damp towel over the animal. That helps lower the body temperature.

2 **An oral syringe** (without needle) is a good way to give your rabbit medicine. Holding the syringe as shown, squirt the medicine slowly into your bunny's mouth from the side.

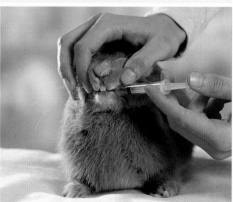

1 **Eyedrops** are dripped carefully into the conjunctival sac. Euphrasia (eyebright), available from the pharmacy, helps for mild inflammations.

3 **Small wounds** heal if you drip some Swedish bitters on them. This remedy acts as a disinfectant and antibiotic.

Snuffles

Not every cold is the dangerous and highly infectious disease known as snuffles. Rabbits with a natural immune deficiency or whose immune system has been weakened by poor husbandry are particularly at risk.

Symptoms: Starts with sneezing, can progress to purulent nasal discharge, labored breathing, bronchitis, ear inflammations, and pneumonia.

Cause: A multifactorial disease. The possibility that a virus is responsible is still under discussion. Bacterial pathogens include *Pasteurella multocida*, *Bordetella bronchiseptica*, and *Staphylococcus*. Infection results from an immune deficiency or contact with other infected rabbits, as well as other house pets. Cannot be transmitted by or to humans!

Treatment: Antibiotics in the early stages, but frequently difficult to cure. Many animals die after a lengthy illness. Vaccination is possible. Basic immunization provided by two shots; an annual booster shot is necessary.

Tip: The vaccine against snuffles is relatively new, but is definitely recommended where available. It must be administered separately (i.e., at a different time) from the vaccines against RHD and myxomatosis.

Heatstroke Costs Lives

In summer we humans enjoy the sun and are glad to see warm weather arrive. Not the rabbit! He wants only one thing now: a cool, breezy spot in the shade. And for good reason. We humans can perspire over our entire bodies to cool ourselves down when we're overheated. Rabbits don't have this ability. A bunny can only try to regulate his body temperature through his ears and by rapid breathing. Wild rabbits in Australia can survive the extreme heat there only because they retreat into their cool underground warrens during the day. Take precautions to make sure your dwarf rabbit doesn't suffer a heatstroke.

▶ In the backyard enclosure and on the balcony, your dwarf rabbits need a large area where it stays cool and shady all day long (see photos, pages 23 and 111). You can also put up a beach umbrella or a "sun tent."

▶ If the shelter or hutch is directly exposed to the midday sun, this can quickly result in heat exhaustion for the animal. It's best to place them in the shade under some trees.

▶ Never transport the animals in a hot car. Reschedule any visits to the veterinarian for the cooler evening hours.

▶ If it's too hot indoors, lay damp towels over the cage roof to promote evaporative cooling. Many rabbits also like to lie on cool tiles.

▶ As a precaution, have your dwarfs with long, dense, angora wool sheared in hot weather (preferably by the veterinarian or at a dog salon).

Symptoms of heatstroke: The animal lies there apathetically, her flanks quivering, nostrils flared, muzzle wet from panting; her head is bent far back (difficulty breathing), and she has a staggering gait, convulsions, and bluish mucosal membranes (circulatory failure).

First aid: Don't waste any time! Get the rabbit into a cool room immediately. Place a damp (not ice-cold) towel over the animal to lower her body temperature (see photo, page 89). A rabbit suffering from heatstroke should receive immediate veterinary care, including fluid therapy.

Tip: Under no circumstance should you give an overheated rabbit a bath or cold shower, or use an ice bag to cool her down.

Danger! Maggots!

Especially at risk: Rabbits in outdoor enclosures, those in a weakened condition, and overweight animals no longer able to groom themselves properly. Even the smallest wound, wet hindquarters, or a bottom smeared with feces will attract flies like magic.

Prevention: Absolute cleanliness in the cage and exercise area is essential during the warm summer months when flies are around. Pick up each one of your dwarf rabbits every day, turn them over carefully, and give them a thorough inspection. Treat even the smallest wound or injury on your rabbit's body at once with Swedish bitters or calendula tincture. This will disinfect and promote wound healing (see photo, page 90). Another alternative is to clean the wound with soapy water.

MY PET

Tubby bunny or racy rabbit?

Almost 40 percent of all dwarf rabbits kept as pets suffer from obesity as a result of improper diet and lack of exercise. Weigh your dwarfs regularly and keep a record.

Here's what you do:

A dwarf rabbit is fully grown at eight months. Weigh the animal at this time, using a kitchen scale (on the floor), for example, and record his starting weight. Check his weight regularly and set up a table. If the dwarf keeps gaining weight, you should devise an exercise program for him (see page 102). If he's clearly losing weight, though, take him to the veterinarian right away.

My test results:

Around the anal area, trim away any fur that is matted with feces or soaked with urine. Then rinse the area with a chamomile solution. Dry it off well, because wet fur holds renewed dangers. Diarrhea patients must be taken to the veterinarian

What can happen: Flies lay their eggs on any soiled, damp, or injured parts of the body. The larvae develop within hours, then burrow into the skin, and can literally eat the poor creature alive. As soon as you find even one tiny maggot on your rabbit, take the affected animal to the veterinarian without delay. If you wait too long, treatment becomes impossible and the only thing left for you to do is put an end to the poor rabbit's suffering.

Treating Minor Ailments Yourself

Diarrhea: Soft stools, soiled anal region, general condition otherwise normal. Give the dwarf nothing except hay to eat and chamomile or fennel tea to drink. Clean the rabbit's quarters carefully and put in fresh bedding. Soft stools can be a sign of a serious problem. A veterinarian should evaluate rabbits with soft or running stools. Remedy any problems with husbandry (drafts, stress, sudden changes in diet). Within one to two days the fecal pellets should appear normal again.

Tip: If this is not the case, or if additional symptoms develop such as apathy or bloated abdomen, please take your dwarf to the veterinarian immediately (bring along a fecal sample).

Measuring temperature: Have the veterinarian show you how to do this before you try it. You can see the correct method in the photo below. Smear the fever thermometer with petroleum jelly before inserting it. That makes it go in more easily. Measure temperature in the anal opening, which is just below the base of the tail. A rabbit's normal body temperature is 101 to 104°F (38.5–40°C).

Administering medicine: The best way to do this is with an oral syringe (without needle). Hold the dwarf rabbit securely and then slowly squirt the medicine into the side of her mouth (see photo, page 90). Don't give her too much at once, or she'll choke. Globules and tablets can also be dissolved in a teaspoon of water first and administered easily this way.

Inhalation: This aids the healing process in respiratory ailments. Place the rabbit on a hand towel in a roomy carrier. Put chamomile flowers or thyme in a heat-proof bowl, pour boiling water over the herbs, and cover both the carrier and the steaming bowl with a light cloth (a bedsheet) (see photo, page 80). Don't use a thick, heavy blanket. Give your bunny inhalation therapy for about 15 minutes two or three times a day.

Tip: Rabbits cannot tolerate inhalants with volatile oils or bronchial remedies containing menthol or eucalyptus. And let me conclude with one more recommendation: Find a good veterinarian, one you trust. Please don't try to be your own veterinarian, and remember that it's better to take your

ailing dwarf rabbit to the doctor once too often rather than too late. You just might save your pet's life this way.

If your rabbit is sick, you should be able to take his temperature. Normal temperature is 101 to 104° (38.5–40°C).

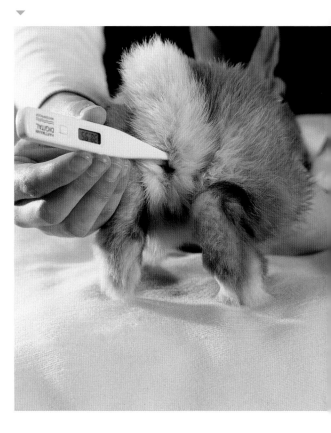

Learning, Training, and Activities

Dwarf rabbits are cheerful, intelligent, and quite capable of learning. But training by force is not their thing. Instead, you should find a variety of ways to stimulate your dwarfs.

What Dwarf Rabbits Can Learn

If you devote a lot of time and attention to your dwarfs, you'll probably be amazed at how clever the little rascals are. Put it to the test and find out how quickly your dwarf rabbits learn.

The dwarf rabbit is not a dog. That's something every rabbit owner must understand. A rabbit does not heel, nor does she fetch on command. Does this mean the dwarf is less intelligent, or merely that she has a mind of her own? How do animals learn, anyway? I'll answer this and other questions for you in the following pages.

Behavior and Learning

Animals, like humans, are lifelong learners. The ability to learn is an important requirement for coping with one's environment and being able to survive there.

Inheritance: Certain patterns of behavior as well as sensory and physical abilities are inherited and need only further training and development. A rabbit doesn't have to learn how to do midair turns, for example. He instinctively puts these abilities to the test even as a youngster so that he can shake off his pursuers later when his life depends on it and not end up in the stomach of a hungry predator.

Hormones: Other behaviors are innate, but are controlled by certain (sex) hormones and don't come into play

until these hormones are produced at sexual maturity. This is the case when bucks who lived together peaceably as youngsters begin fighting for social dominance as they reach sexual maturity, or when a pregnant doe collects straw in her mouth and plucks out her belly wool to build a warm nest in preparation for the birth of her offspring.

Socialization phase: Young rabbits, like other mammals, go through a so-called socialization phase. In rabbits this lasts until about the 12th week of life. What youngsters experience during this period has a lasting influence on the

A cat-litter box ▶
with a rim, filled
with straw pellets,
helps with litter-
box training.

▶ 1 **Tie a carrot** to a string and use it to coax the rabbit very slowly through a house or tunnel. This works best if the dwarf trusts you.

▶ 2 **Stairs** made of aircrete are easy to cut and are impregnated with nontoxic pigment. They are a great way to practice climbing.

▶ 3 **Cover food bowls** with green and red cardboard. Can your dwarf tell which one conceals the treat?

rest of their lives. That's why it is so important for pet rabbits to receive loving care from their humans right from the start. Young animals raised this way are already "hand-tame" when they are put up for adoption at eight weeks and have been positively imprinted on humans. Youngsters that have not been socialized, on the other hand, need lots of patience and love to become truly friendly. If there have been negative experiences, a timid, nervous mother, or an unfavorable genetic makeup, then in most cases future behavioral problems are preprogrammed.

Further learning: From now on, everything the rabbit learns over the course of her life influences her behavior. Like every other living creature, the rabbit tries to have "good, positive feelings" and avoid "unpleasant, painful feelings" whenever possible. The rabbit can remember and is able to associate events and her own behavior with the experiences and feelings

resulting from them. Thus a wild rabbit will always return eagerly to a place where she finds the tastiest grasses and herbs—a positive experience and association. If, however, a colony of wild rabbits is pursued by hunters or constantly threatened by people out walking their dogs, these wild rabbits will react to even a "harmless" stroller with panicky flight. That's because they associate painful and life-threatening experiences with all approaching humans. Our dwarf rabbits behave in a similar manner. If the animal receives tasty tidbits from your outstretched hand, if you pet him gently and treat him kindly, then a positive association is formed and the animal learns, "This hand is good to me, and so is this person." If, on the other hand, you run up to your dwarf rabbit or grab him from above without warning like a bird of prey, he'll remember that. In the future, the rabbit will associate you and your hand with his negative feelings. He has learned, "This hand hurts me, this

person frightens me." If your dwarf rabbit is especially easygoing, he will probably forgive you if you make a mistake. But an animal that is already frightened and rather shy will either become even more withdrawn or will behave aggressively toward you in self-defense.

The Self-reliant rabbit

Munchkin is the smallest member of my rabbit community, but he's also the smartest. He catches on fast. Not long ago I was in the midst of preparing a vegetable lasagna. The chopped vegetables were already lying in front of me on the table when the telephone rang in the hall. My best friend had something important to tell me. When I returned to the kitchen half an hour later, Munchkin was sitting on the table devouring the last of the vegetables with obvious enjoyment. The little rascal had jumped up on a kitchen chair and from there to the table. Since then I don't dare leave Munchkin unsupervised in the kitchen during his free-roaming time. That marvelous food source "kitchen table" is a constant temptation.

TIP

Learning through rewards

The rabbit is motivated and induced to learn when you reward her, for example with a treat. Enjoyment and other pleasant feelings should always be associated with the desired behavior. Fear, on the other hand, will block her response and lead to avoidance behavior.

Can Rabbits Be Trained?

Who wouldn't like to have rabbits that obeyed commands and, of course, used the litter box? Many dwarfs can successfully complete a little training course, but others prefer to remain "true" rabbits in every way.

Especially when rabbits are kept indoors, conflicts arise between the needs and natural behaviors of the rabbit and those of the owner. Not every animal can be trained to be a "good" house rabbit.

Every Rabbit Is Different

In Chapter 3, page 56, I gave you the most important guidelines for getting along with your rabbit. They form the foundation for any future training. When you are training or interacting with your rabbits, it's also helpful to pay close attention to their individual differences.

The impudent rascal: He usually hops through life full of confidence. In a community this rabbit likes to be the boss or queen bee. Rascals are adventurous, can even be taught little tricks, and like to be the center of attention. You could describe them as a mixture of charmer and wise guy. Somewhat obstinate and downright sly, these rabbits manage to trick us time and again. Before we realize what's happened, the dwarf has trained us instead of us training the dwarf (see Who's training whom here?, right).

The touch-me-not: She is cautious and shy in everything. If this rabbit lives with others, she rarely hops first in line, but prefers to follow instead. Touch-me-nots are no less intelligent, but they're easily rattled and overwhelmed by changes. If you have a dwarf like this at home, then bear in mind that she needs a bit more time to learn something and a very gentle hand when being trained. If a touch-me-not has learned to trust her human and feels safe and secure, she can become especially affectionate and cuddly.

Who's Training Whom Here?

That's what I ask myself when I think of my foster rabbit, the little wise guy Spunky. Spunky insists on being fed punctually—and I insist on sleeping late on the weekend. When Spunky was brought to me, he settled in right away. Before long he noticed that two mornings a week he got his food a bit later than usual. Oh, well, I thought, Spunky just has to get used to it. But I hadn't reckoned on my clever dwarf rabbit. One Sunday morning I heard a racket in my "rabbit room." What was going on? I jumped out of bed to investigate, and what did I see there? Spunky had the stainless steel bowl from the exercise pen in his little mouth and was flinging it around the enclosure as if to say, "When's breakfast?" Ever

▲

Houseplants should be out of reach for your dwarf rabbit indoors.

since then, I use only heavy ceramic bowls, and Spunky gets his meals punctually, even on the weekend.

Coming When Called . . . or Not

Coaxing a rabbit to "come" with a treat is really quite simple—provided the rabbit trusts us, is hungry at the moment, and isn't busy doing something more "important." Don't expect your pet to come when called like a dog. It's better if you keep a sense of humor and try to think up a better solution. Here's how you can train a rabbit to come:

Hand-feeding: Late mornings after the breakfast hay and evenings before the second meal are the best times to hand-feed your rabbit greens and fresh fruits and vegetables (dandelion greens, grass, parsley, carrot, apple). In the beginning, hold out the food to her in her cage and wait until she comes over. Later you can lie down on the floor of the enclosure and repeat feeding her by hand.

Coaxing Voice: Get into the habit of using a coaxing tone of voice. Rabbits don't understand our human language, of course, but they certainly do notice the friendly tone of voice. On the other hand, the animals dislike bossy commands as well as shrill sounds and nervous behavior. If you keep several rabbits, you'll soon discover that the animals don't answer to a specific name. They can, however, notice characteristic sounds associated with your tone of voice. For example, say,

"Come, carrot, yummy" or "Hmmm, food, Freddy" or simply, "Come, come, Hannibal."

Tip: Practice with your dwarf rabbits when they have the greatest incentive to come to you. If a rabbit has already eaten his fill, for example, or is taking a little break or is busy doing something more "important" like taking a bath, digging holes, or snuggling with his

patient and persevere. Many dwarf rabbits can at least be litter-box trained to some extent. For the "problem cases," I've collected a few tips for you in Chapter 8, page 129.

Try this: If the rabbits use one corner of their cage as their natural latrine, you can put a plastic tray there and fill it with small-animal litter or straw pellets. I strongly advise against using any kind of cat-litter product, because they are harmful for rabbits. Watch your dwarfs to be sure they don't chew on the

DID YOU KNOW THAT . . .

. . . learning ability decreases under too much stress?

Modern research examines the influence of stress on cognitive ability (recognition, comprehension, perception) in humans and animals. Stress hormones can increase cognitive ability up to a point. However, as soon as stress exceeds a certain level, errors in perception occur more and more frequently. Rabbits, too, learn better in a relaxed atmosphere and without pressure to perform.

rabbit buddies, then your prospects for success are rather slim.

How Can Dwarf Rabbits Be Trained to Use the Litter Box?

Rabbits are by nature clean animals. This is actually a good first step for training them to use the litter box. If only they didn't have their marking behavior, i.e., the need to indicate their territory with aromatic droppings (see page 20). But don't lose heart! Be

plastic; if they do, you'll have to remove the litter box.

I no longer use a litter box in my animals' cage except during their exercise period. When my dwarfs are enjoying this free-roaming time, I leave the cage door open so they can use this litter box if they need it.

In the beginning, limit the exercise area and don't let your rabbits roam through the whole house right away. That would be expecting too much of the animals. Rabbits prefer to defecate and urinate in corners and dark hiding places. Set up

Many dwarfs never learn to use a litter box despite **all attempts** attempts at training them. Take it in stride and don't punish the animal.

the litter boxes in spots the animals—not you—have chosen.

I use standard large cat-litter boxes with a rim or a hood, but no entrance flap. The little rascals can dig in there, too, without scattering litter all over the room (see photo, page 95).

To help your rabbits understand what the box is for, gather a few fecal pellets and some straw from the "bathroom corner" in the cage and place them in the litter box.

Watch your dwarf rabbits closely. If an animal looks like she's about to pee somewhere—she'll start to lift her hindquarters slightly—say sharply and distinctly, "No!" or "Yuck!" Then carefully lead the animal to the litter box, but please don't chase her! You don't want her to regard the box as a prison. You can pick up a trusting rabbit and place her in the box. If any droppings land where they shouldn't, put them in the box as soon as possible or vacuum them up. Remove urine spots on the carpet right away. Peppermint oil or lemon oil in water masks the odor of urine and discourages the dwarf from peeing in this spot again. You can also buy commercial products designed to eliminate urine odor and stains at a pet store or through an online vendor.

Don't use ammonia. It is very similar to urine. If the animal does her business in the litter box, praise her lovingly: "Good!" A reward will also help the "business." Remember the positive associations (see Tip, page 97).

It goes without saying that you should never shout at a rabbit or give her a smack on the rump as punishment. Not only would this be unfair, but it would achieve exactly the opposite result, because a dwarf rabbit who's upset will certainly never learn to use the litter box.

A cardboard tube studded with pellets makes an enjoyable chew toy for the rabbit.
▼

Things Are Hopping Here!

Dwarf rabbits need an enriched environment with plenty of variety.
Here they can enjoy life with other rabbits and exhibit many different kinds of behavior.
You'll be in demand as a playmate, too, if you spend time with your dwarfs.

Body and mind need stimulation and activity in equal measure. This is as true for our rabbits as it is for us humans. Boredom, on the other hand, makes us dull and ill.

Exercise Course

Slipping through tunnels, hiding, jumping on or over small obstacles, digging: All these things are fun for rabbits and keep the little rascals fit.

Cardboard boxes: The main thing is that they're sturdy so they can't tip over and so the rabbits can jump on the top without breaking through. Cut a variety of doorways in the boxes so you can make an entire playground for them.

Cozy box: Put a thick layer of newspaper on the bottom of a fruit crate; it will absorb urine in case the rabbit happens to "misuse" the box. Then fill the crate with loose balls of paper towels, paper napkins, or toilet paper. Rabbits love to snuggle in the heaps of paper and can also nibble on the wooden fruit crate. In the fall I fill boxes or crates with fragrant dried leaves for a little variety.

Cork tubes: These are made from the bark of the cork oak, can be chewed, and are available in all sizes at the pet store. Buy tubes at least 6⅓ inches (16 cm) in diameter that are shaped so they will rest on the floor (see photo, page 40).

Crinkle tunnel: These tunnels are made of washable synthetic fabric and are available in the pet store. Some crinkle tunnels can be laid end to end; others can even be snapped together to make an arch. It's a clever idea, actually, provided your rabbits—like mine— don't chew on it. If they do start to nibble it, switch to natural products.

Digging box: Rabbits naturally love to dig in dirt, sand, or a mixture of the two. Both are inexpensive and available at home improvement stores or garden centers (don't use soil containing fertilizer!). Of course, you can also build a wooden box. I find this too involved, too heavy, and too difficult to keep clean. Instead, I use standard cat-litter boxes as digging boxes, either open with a rim, or with a hood but no entrance flap (see photo, page 40). Fill the bottom tray (16 x 20 inches [40 x 50 cm]) with a layer of sand 3 inches (7 cm) deep. If you like, you can place a stone slab beneath the sand to let your bunnies wear down their toenails. My rabbits dig in these boxes, roll around in them, and enjoy their midday naps there, too.

Tunnel system: I tried this a few days ago in my rabbit's exercise pen. My verdict: What a hit! The system consists of a crinkle tunnel and two cork tubes with different diameters (see text, left) that are linked together securely. One end of the crinkle tunnel lies in a digging box (cat-litter box with hood). The other end of the tunnel system opens in a fruit crate that I have set up as a cozy box (see text, left). To make sure the tunnel stays put, I sawed out the wooden slats of the fruit crate in one spot. In the middle of the crinkle tunnel there is an additional hole through which my dwarfs can run out and jump over the tunnel.

Hurdles: If you're not much of a handyman, you can just set up a row of tin cans (see photo, page 107). If you're a do-it-yourselfer, you should keep three things in mind: Don't make it too high—5 to 7 inches (14–18 cm) is adequate for a dwarf rabbit; you're not getting into competitive sports here, just providing some rabbit-friendly exercise. The hurdles must be stable (i.e., have a large base plate) so they don't fall over right away. The animals prefer jumping over longer obstacles, about a yard (meter) in length, rather than shorter ones. I place the hurdles in the middle of the enclosure and put a small hut and a cardboard box nearby. The hurdles act like natural obstacles and the dwarfs jump over them on their own. Even my six-week-old "youngsters" join in enthusiastically.

"Working" for Food Keeps Them Fit and Healthy

In the wild, rabbits have to search for their food and really stretch to reach those tasty twigs. Always having everything served in their food bowls gets to be a bit boring after a while, even for dwarf rabbits. For some time now, zookeepers have been working on activity programs in which the animals have to search for their food and work to get it, similar to their natural behavior in the wild.

Rabbits love raised lookouts. This hanging bridge is perfect outdoors.
▼

HAZARDS FOR YOUR DWARF RABBITS

If your dwarf rabbits roam freely, you must take a few precautions.

Hazard	What can happen	Remedy
Electrical cords	electric shock if the rabbit chews on it	Put it under the carpet or baseboard.
Doors	rabbit could get caught and be injured	Open and close doors carefully.
Smooth floors	rabbit slips, gets hurt	Put carpeting or a maize/coir mat in the exercise area.
Tables/chairs	rabbit could fall off	Never put the animal on a chair or table and leave him unattended.
Plants	could be poisonous if eaten	Never rely on the animal's instincts; remove cacti and poisonous plants (see Internet addresses, page 141).
Cleaning products	could be poisonous if eaten or swallowed	Store out of reach.
Plastic	can cause intestinal blockage if chewed	Watch what rabbit nibbles on; keep plastic objects out of reach.
Dogs/cats	can cause stress/shock if they chase rabbit; bite wounds	Never let them out together without supervision.
People	If rabbit runs between your legs, you could step on her.	Move very carefully; always look down/behind.
Predators	can kill rabbits	Protect the enclosure, even on the balcony.

Toy dice: Made of wood or sisal, toy dice are sold in pet stores for hamsters. If you fill them with hay, they make a great chew toy for rabbits (see photo, page 107).

Hay sock: Surely you have an old cotton sock that you can get rid of. Stuff it with hay, as shown in the photo below, and hang it by a string in the cage or pen.

Porcupine chew toy: Stick some herb pellets or hay cubes in a paper-towel tube. The animals love to roll this porcupine chew toy around, and it keeps them busy for a long time (see photo, page 101.)

Food necklace: Using a sturdy needle, string together a variety of treats (apple, fennel, lettuce leaf, carrot, see photo, page 72). The necklace can be strung up in the enclosure so that the rabbits have to stretch to nibble on it. You can also tie together some fresh herbs or a bunch of dandelion greens and hang them up for your dwarfs.

Veggie kebab: Skewer some greens and fresh veggies on a barbecue spit and stick this in the top of a box or basket. The rabbits have to climb up on top so they can nibble on it. You can also spear everything on a thin twig and wedge it overhead in the cage wire.

Snack ball: This is a plastic ball with an adjustable opening, available from the pet store. When the rabbit rolls it around, treats fall out. Please don't fill it with unhealthful treats; instead use dried vegetables and fruit.

Twigs: Stick twigs with leaves and/or buds in a brick or wedge them in the cage wires overhead. A real treat to chew!

Chewing log: I developed this chewing log eight years ago; it's still in use and has been copied or modified by many rabbit owners (see photos, pages 33 and 40). A forked tree trunk is screwed into

Dwarf rabbits need **activities** to be happy as pets.

a plywood board ½ inch (12 mm) thick with a diameter of 16 inches (40 cm) (no smaller, otherwise it will tip over!). For dwarf rabbits, I recommend a

To keep your dwarfs entertained, stuff a cotton sock with hay and hang it overhead. ▶

height of 11 to 13½ inches (28–34 cm). A trunk thickness of 4¾ inches (12 cm) lets you drill deep holes for hiding treats: narrow holes for greens, bigger ones for carrots, and a deep hole on the top for twigs. Starting at 4 inches (10 cm) from the bottom, I've drilled a variety of holes in the trunk. This way both youngsters and full-grown dwarfs can have fun with the treat log.

Decorating Ideas for the Outdoor Enclosure

Outdoors the furnishing must be weatherproof and provide cool shade in the summer.

Hollow log: The next time you go for a walk in the woods, bring back a tree trunk with a rotten center. The soft, decaying wood can easily be scraped out. Next smooth the interior again with an electric sander or by hand, and your rabbits will have a fantastic weatherproof natural den (see photos, pages 40, 44, and 111).

Drainpipes: These are available in home improvement centers or building supply stores and can be covered with dirt or sand. To make sure it's cool inside for the rabbits in summer, you should buy ceramic pipes rather than plastic ones.

Hanging bridge: I designed the bridge exclusively for this handbook, and you can easily build one like it yourself. Screw four small tree trunks, 16 inches (40 cm) tall, about 2 inches (5 cm) in diameter, to a solid wood board, 28 inches (70 cm) long, 16 inches (40 cm) wide, and ¾ inch (20 mm) thick. The large willow bridge (20 inches [50 cm] long, 14 inches [35 cm] wide) is from

the pet store, and you can attach it securely to the four tree trunks with screws or wire. Make sure it doesn't wobble, because the rabbits don't like that! If you wish, you can even decorate the whole thing with twigs to chew on. Your rabbits will love this elevated perch, and it's very pretty, besides (see photos, pages 36 and 103).

Willow tent: I found this tent in a garden center. It's made of willow canes woven together with poles. The dwarfs can always find an airy spot of shade here under the tent, even in the middle of summer (see photos, pages 46 and 111).

Leafy tepee: As I was watching wild rabbits outside under the bushes, I decided to construct something similar for the exercise pen. Place a section of wood planking (available in a garden center) on four stone blocks. Above this fasten leafy branches together to form a tent. The rabbits can snuggle beneath this leafy tepee, slip through it, or nibble on the twigs to their heart's content (see photo, page 23).

Garden edging: I also found this in the garden center. The edging consists of split wooden posts held together with wire. You can set it up as a little labyrinth in the backyard enclosure (see photo, page 111), or you can place it as shown on page 46 to make a bridge between the two movable pens.

Tree stumps: Rabbits like to use these as raised lookouts (thick roots, too).

An amphora: Lined with hay, it makes a snug, weatherproof retreat (see photo, page 32).

2 **Hurdles** for daily exercise don't have to be elaborate. A series of unopened tin cans works, too; as you can see, the Mini Lop hops over it enthusiastically.

1 **A sisal ball** filled with hay is a safe treat the dwarf rabbits can roll around and nibble on.

3 **A shoe box** filled with paper makes a great crinkle box. The rabbits can "dig" and hide in it.

Can I Teach My Dwarfs Tricks?

Teaching your rabbits tricks not only gives them something to do during their out-of-cage time, but also strengthens the bond between you and your little companions. Don't begin, though, until the animals have learned to trust you and come to you when you call (see page 99).

Periscope bunny

This is actually part of the rabbit's natural behavioral repertoire. But now you can teach him to do it on command. Here's how:

▸ Hold a treat such as a sprig of parsley in front of the dwarf's nose.

▸ If he wants to nibble on it, raise the parsley very slowly until he's sitting on his hind legs to reach the treat.

▸ Associate the exercise with the word "*Up!*"

▸ As a reward for standing on his hind legs, your "periscope bunny" naturally gets the parsley right away.

▸ Repeat the exercise several times until your bunny has learned to associate the command with the reward.

▸ Eventually many rabbits even learn to sit up when given a hand signal along with the word "*Up!*"

The Wandering Carrot

In this simple food game, you tie a carrot to a string and lay it in front of the rabbit's nose. If she wants to nibble

◄ *A pile of sand in the outdoor pen makes a great playground for these enthusiastic diggers.*

on it, pull the treat very slowly toward you. If the dwarf rabbit follows her carrot, reward her with a bite of it when she reaches her "goal." You can also drag the treat through a tunnel, a box, or a house (see photo, page 96). This exercise only works if the animal is hungry enough, though.

Into the basket

Children often have trouble picking up their rabbits and carrying them safely. That's why I recommend "basket transport" (see page 57). It's most pleasant for the rabbit if he learns to jump into the basket by himself and remain sitting there. Here's how to get your pet used to this:

▶ Tip the basket on its side and put some food in it so the rabbit can check it out.
▶ If the rabbit takes the food out of the basket, coax him over next time with the command "*Basket!*"
▶ Now set the basket upright. If the rabbit jumps in on command, reward him with the food and an affectionate pat.
▶ Now you can safely pick up the rabbit in the basket and carry him. Go only short distances at first, and for safety's sake always keep one hand on the animal's back.

MY PET

Can dwarfs distinguish colors? How smart are they?

Scientific tests have shown that rabbits probably can't distinguish colors very well. It's likely that the animals see only red or green as different shades of gray.

The test begins:

Set up two food bowls. Place a green piece of cardboard over one and a red piece over the other (see photo, page 97). Only the bowl with the green cover contains food. Can your rabbit discover this and push the cover away? Repeat the test, but switch the places of the bowls. The food always stays in the bowl with the green cover. Which rabbit can remember this?

My test results:

Questions on
Learning, Training, and Activities

My dwarf always sits around in her exercise pen looking bored even though I've furnished it so nicely for her. Why is that?

If your rabbit is otherwise healthy, it could be that she's lonely. Rabbits are social animals; they hop around much more in the exercise pen if there are two of them and communicate with each other. Try to find another rabbit as a companion for your pet. But you should also spend time with her regularly and, if she enjoys it, cuddle with her, too, sometimes.

My little bucks Max and Moritz are allowed to run around all day in their backyard enclosure, but at night they have to go into their safe hutch because of the weasels. Often they don't want to, though, and they won't let me catch them.

Can you suggest any helpful tricks?

Whatever you do, don't chase after your rabbits. This is just stressful for all concerned. It's better if you can persuade the animals to go into their hutch at night on their own. Try this: Leave the hutch door open and coax the little rascals over with a tasty treat that you've placed in their house. Then give them the command, "*Come, house!*" Be patient, because they first have to learn that their hutch is not a prison where they'll be locked up. From now on it will be a cozy home where fragrant hay, succulent greens, and fresh foods await them. Start giving them their evening meal in the hutch only. Try, also, to train the animals when you have plenty of time, not when you're in a hurry. Rabbits can tell when you're stressed, and then in most cases they won't cooperate at all.

My name is Tina and I am 12 years old. I have two sweet Lionhead rabbits who have a bad habit: They gnaw on the baseboards. How can I get my rabbits to stop doing this?

All rabbits gnaw and chew with a passion. Give your pets twigs and plenty of hay regularly so they have lots of opportunities to chew. Other than that, you have to watch the two of them carefully. As soon as one begins to gnaw on the baseboard, clap your hands and shout, "No!" If the rabbit stops, praise him and pet him. Rabbits are not dumb, and they're definitely capable of learning.

Recently I heard of a type of sport called "rabbit hopping." This is supposed to be some sort of agility training for rabbits. What's your opinion of it?

Would you recommend "rabbit hopping"?

I don't recommend "rabbit hopping," nor do I think it's a suitable activity for and with rabbits. In "rabbit hopping" a rabbit on a leash jumps over hurdles that are built up with rails (similar to equestrian show jumping). Even though these rails can fall down if necessary and the rabbit wears an additional jumping harness, the risk of injury to my dwarfs would be much too great for me. Besides, although rabbits can indeed jump high in an emergency, their body is designed more for hopping, running, or jumping over low obstacles. The long drive to the rabbit-hopping event, the unfamiliar people and noises, and the barren field without cover all mean stress pure and simple for a territorial, sedentary flight animal. I recommend you set up a little exercise course in your own home for your dwarf rabbits (see page 102). Here your animals can jump, hop around, and have lots of fun in familiar surroundings, totally relaxed and without a leash.

? **My dwarf rabbit Speedy is four months old. Until now, Speedy has done his "business" like a good bunny in his cage and in his litter box. But lately he urinates and defecates in various spots around the house. Why is he doing that now?**

Your Speedy has become sexually mature and is now starting to mark his territory with aromatic fecal pellets. Before long he might begin to spray urine, too. I recommend that you have your buck castrated as soon as possible by an experienced veterinarian (see Neutering, page 85). Castrated male rabbits are usually better about using their litter boxes.

? **I've taught my rabbits a few tricks, but they quickly lose interest in training. Why do you think that is?**

Rabbits don't play tirelessly for long periods like dogs, who will still chase after a ball enthusiastically the tenth time you throw it. Rabbits usually lose interest in an exercise after the second or third repetition. Sometimes even the tastiest motivational aid can't tempt them. The fun determines the length of the game. This also guarantees that the animals are not overtaxed. Simply take an occasional break when you're training. After that, practice some more. The dwarfs might come up to you and prefer to cuddle, or maybe they'd rather snuggle with their bunny buddies, or maybe they just have something more "important" to do.

Family Planning and Raising Young

Young dwarf rabbits are among the cutest animal babies I know. Nevertheless, you should consider carefully whether you can offer all these youngsters a good home.

New Additions to Your Rabbit Family

If you would like to raise rabbits, you need plenty of room. Even at three weeks of age, the youngsters want to explore the surroundings outside their nest, hop and jump around in the exercise pen, and practice standing on their hind legs.

Wild rabbits are the prey of countless predators. Only their enormous fertility lets them compensate for their high mortality rate and so ensure the survival of their species. What contributes to ecological balance in the wild, though, becomes our responsibility when we keep rabbits as pets.

Unexpected Offspring

I know from letters and conversations that many rabbit marriages are arranged in secret. Without their parents' knowledge, school friends and their rabbits get together and, partly for fun and partly out of childish curiosity, try to find out where baby rabbits come from. Be sure to explain this to your children right from the start. Other owners, though, are surprised to find rabbit babies in the nest one morning when two supposed does turn out to be a male and a female. When you get young rabbits, never rely exclusively on the say-so of one person. If you want to play it safe, you should always consult a second expert, for example a veterinarian or experienced breeder (see text page 53, photo, page 55).

Neutering performed at the appropriate time also prevents unwanted offspring (see page 85).

Preparations for Starting a Family

If you have decided to mate your rabbits and raise their young, I have some suggestions for you:
The parents: Both should be in excellent health and have no physical abnormalities. If one parent, for example, has a congenital malocclusion, this will be passed on to their progeny! Because temperament also has an

A Mini Lop, ▶ five weeks old, snuggles together with a Netherland Dwarf, three weeks old.

1 **The buck circles** around the doe as part of the mating ritual. If the doe is not yet ready to mate, the buck will continue to court his intended.

2 **During copulation** the doe raises her rump slightly and the buck mounts her and holds on.

3 **After ejaculation** the buck falls off the doe with a short grunt and lies there exhausted.

influence on the offspring, I mate only dwarf rabbits who are trusting, friendly, and even tempered. The ideal breeding age is from eight months to four years. Although it's true that rabbits are sexually mature by three months of age, mating a doe too early can cause her physical harm.

Housing: A rabbit family needs plenty of room. An extra-large cage measuring 57 x 32 inches (145 x 80 cm) is ideal for the mother and her babies. I let my doe move into the two-story condo, and the little family loved it (see page 34).

When Is the Doe Willing to Mate?

The doe's readiness to mate is called estrus, or "heat." It is controlled by hormones and influenced by various environmental factors such as day length (photoperiod), outside temperature, and food supply. Rabbits kept indoors can be in heat almost all year long. You can tell when a doe is ready to mate because she immediately lifts her hindquarters when you stroke her rump. The labia of her vulva are slightly reddened and swollen. Her behavior also changes at this time. She begins to paw around more in the bedding and becomes more aggressive toward rival does. This is in keeping with her natural instincts and has nothing to do with "bad" behavior.

Tip: Because I am often asked this by readers: Female rabbits do not experience monthly bleeding (menstruation).

Rabbit Nuptials

You can best observe the wide range of behaviors associated with mating if you let animals who are already acquainted with each other mate in a roomy pen. If the doe is ready to mate, everything can happen very quickly. Otherwise, the male continues to court his intended until she finally pays attention to him (see photos, above).

Sniffing and marking: The male sniffs the anal region of the doe, picking up her exciting scent in the process, and can then tell how receptive she is to mating. He resumes marking his territory by rubbing vigorously with his chin glands (chinning). Some bucks spray the female with a well-aimed stream of urine and in this way mark their sweetheart!

Circling: When the doe sits or lies down, the buck displays by circling her with a stiff-legged gait. As he does this he raises his tail high against his back and shows the doe the light underside of his tail (the "scut"). In technical terms, this behavior is called tail flagging. It's assumed that the buck gives off a sexual aroma from the exposed glandular ducts.

Caressing: If the doe is not yet ready to mate, the two like to lie with their heads close together and the male licks her affectionately. If the male interrupts his courtship behavior, the female may nudge him with her muzzle, as if to say, "Caress me some more."

Chasing: The doe allows the buck to come closer, but as soon as he starts to get "pushy," she quickly hops away. Then the female does some twisty midair leaps, always making sure he sees her. When I watch this playful chase, I have to smile. It reminds me of the first adolescent games between girls

TIP

The lady comes to the gentleman

If the breeding pair doesn't live together, you must bring the doe to the buck when she is in heat. It doesn't work the other way around, since the doe will defend her territory vigorously. And the "gentleman" is too unsure of himself in unfamiliar surroundings to carry out his task.

and boys, a mixture of interest and feigned rejection.

Copulation: If the male's efforts have stimulated the female sufficiently, she lies down quietly and lifts her rump so the buck can penetrate more easily. He mounts her, biting his chosen one in the neck and clasping her with his front legs, and then with a rapid series of copulatory movements expels the

Important tip: If you don't want any more offspring, the buck should be castrated right away; after castration, he should be housed separately from the doe for another six weeks to be on the safe side. It's possible that any sperm still present could lead to another fertilization. The doe, too, is able to conceive immediately after birth.

DID YOU KNOW THAT . . .

. . . rabbit's milk is a health tonic?

A mother rabbit's milk contains almost four times as much fat, protein, and minerals as cow's milk. Only sugar content is lower: 4.6 percent in cow's milk compared with just 0.9 percent in rabbit's milk. That's why orphaned baby rabbits can be raised only with a special lactose-reduced milk replacer. In their first two to three days, newborn rabbits drink the so-called colostrum, which has a high concentration of antibodies (immunoglobulins) and protects the babies against disease. Although the doe nurses her young only once to at most twice a day, and then only for a few minutes each time, the babies have doubled their birth weight after just one week. This is astonishing if you consider how often and how long mother cats and dogs nurse their offspring in comparison.

sperm (ejaculation). After successful copulation, the male slides off the doe—usually with a short grunt—and lies there for a few seconds, exhausted. Ovulation is triggered about 10 to 12 hours later, and the eggs are fertilized by sperm waiting in the oviducts.

Make sure you give the pregnant doe
plenty of nesting material
in the form of fresh straw.

The Pregnant Doe

From the day of fertilization to birth, the doe carries her young for an average of 31 days (28 to 33 are possible). If you were present at mating, you should note down this date. This way you can calculate the expected time of birth and prepare for it better. Many expectant mothers are more aggressive toward other rabbits and may be more nervous and snappish toward you as well. Be sympathetic, because the doe is only following her natural protective instincts. It doesn't have to be this way, though. When caring for a pregnant doe, there are a few rules you must follow and some preparations you need to make.

Quiet: The doe gets her own home; until her young are put up for adoption, it must not be moved or changed. You should also avoid lifting her and carrying her around. If the doe lives with one or more rabbits in the group, watch the mother to see if she still likes the interaction or feels stressed by it. Many pregnant females continue to enjoy the company of castrated males, at least in the exercise area, although you still have to keep them separated after castration (see page 85).

The last week of pregnancy: Now you should clean the cage thoroughly again and spread plenty of fresh straw so the doe can build her nest. A mother rabbit may begin busily collecting straw in her mouth before this and use it to furnish the nest. A few days before she gives birth (called "kindling"), although sometimes not until that day, the doe pulls out her loose belly fur and uses it to line the nest. Don't be surprised if the doe fills up the kindling box completely with straw (see Kindling box, page 118). Many owners worry that the young won't get enough air inside. I have always had confidence in my does, and so far not one of their babies has suffocated.

Tip: On the last days before the kindling date, you should leave the doe in her cage. This guarantees she'll drop her young in the nest and not somewhere in the exercise area if labor begins suddenly.

_____

The pregnant doe will appreciate a kindling box like this where she can build her nest.
▼

This 18-day-old dwarf is no bigger than the palm of your hand; as an altricial animal, he is completely dependent on his mother's care.

The kindling box

Wild rabbits raise their offspring in underground dens. You can accommodate your doe's needs by offering her a kindling box. My does always accept these gratefully. The kindling box also has a practical advantage. If a doe simply builds her nest in the bedding out in the open, then you have to be very careful later on when cleaning the cage that you don't damage her carefully constructed nest or that one of the tiny babies doesn't get lost in the bedding. It's best if you put the kindling box in the doe's cage right after mating. I always spread a layer of small-animal bedding (untreated softwood shavings) 1 inch (3 cm) deep on the floor and over this put a layer of straw about 3 inches (7 cm)

deep. I leave the rest of the work up to the doe.

Instructions for building the kindling box: These dimensions are appropriate for a female dwarf or a Mini Lop. The kindling box is 9¾ inches (25 cm) high, 8¼ inches (21 cm) wide, and 16 inches (41 cm) long. The cover can be pushed back and slides between two strips of wood. This makes it easier to check on the babies later. The floor and long sides are closed. The rear panel is only 8½ inches (22 cm) high, the remaining 1¼ inches (3 cm) being left open. There is an entrance in the front for the doe. To prevent the babies from crawling out of the nest too soon, the bottom 5½ inches (14 cm) of the doorway is covered by a board. The opening above this, 4¼ inches (11 cm) high, is more than enough for the doe. I recommend you use ¼-inch (5 mm) thick beech plywood if you keep the rabbit indoors, and ½-inch (10 mm) thick exterior-grade plywood for outdoors. To protect the babies, I don't apply a finish (see photo, page 117).

Birth ("Kindling")

The doe usually brings her young into the world so quickly and quietly that you might not even be aware of it. For dwarf rabbits, the average litter size is four young, plus or minus two. Immediately after birth, the doe cleans the helpless newborns (called kits) with her tongue, severs the umbilical cords, and eats the afterbirths so that the nest stays clean. Shortly afterward, the kits begin suckling the nourishing colostrum from their mother's nipples for the first time.

Development of the Young
At a Glance

◀ The first days

These two dwarfs are eight days old. Their initial birth weight has now doubled. They are beginning to open their eyes and to hear, and you can make out the future color of their fur.

iscovering the world ▶

t four weeks things are etting lively. Outside in the en, the youngsters sniff nd nibble at everything nd do wild leaps in the air. low is the time to form a rusting relationship.

At three weeks

Their birth weight has quadrupled, and the youngsters now have their soft baby fur. The first ones leave the nest, nibble on hay, and practice standing on their hind legs.

Almost independent ▶

After six weeks, the gastrointestinal tract of the youngsters has adjusted completely to solid food. They still nurse occasionally, though, and need to be together. At seven to eight weeks, they can be put up for adoption.

◀ *This tricolor Mini Lop is just ten weeks old. Soon he'll be sexually mature and will begin fighting to establish dominance.*

Inspecting the nest: Coax the doe with a treat to leave her house and go into her exercise area. While she's running around, you can give the kits their first checkup without interruption. To do this, open the nest carefully, check to see if every one of the babies is alive and uninjured, and count the litter. You must remove any remnants of the afterbirth or dead kits. Also check the bedding in the rest of the cage to see if any kits were dropped there. If this is the case, you must put the poor little thing in the warm nest right away; otherwise it will die of hypothermia and starvation. A mother rabbit won't carry her kit back into the nest the way mother cats and dogs do.

Development of the Young

As typical altricial animals, rabbits come into the world naked, blind, and deaf. Only their senses of smell and touch are developed. They cannot regulate their body temperature themselves, so they snuggle close to each other in their warmly lined nest where the temperature stays around 95°F (35°C). The doe visits her kits to nurse once or at most twice a day. When she squats down, the kits are at her nipples in a flash and nurse lying on their backs (see page 118). After each feeding, the doe licks the kits' bellies, thus stimulating their intestinal activity, and eats their droppings so that the nest stays clean.

On the fifth day: Their skin, naked at first, is now covered with velvety fur. You can already get an idea of the future coat color.

After a week: Birth weight has doubled.

Days 9 to 11: Eyes and ears open, and the dwarfs see and hear. First movement of the ears can be observed.

At two weeks: The youngsters now have a dense, fuzzy baby coat and are crawling around the kindling box. Their birth weight has quadrupled. You can observe their first tentative attempts at grooming, although the youngsters still have problems with balance.

In the third week of life: Now the first youngsters begin to leave the kindling box. They hop around the cage and practice standing up on their hind legs without falling over. The young dwarf rabbits nibble inquisitively at stalks of hay. By the end of the third week, the doe's milk production is slowly declining.

Weeks four to five: Now the place is hopping, and at my house the kits are allowed to leave their two-story condo and join the others in the exercise pen. My castrated bucks behave very affectionately, snuggle with the kits, and groom them. The rascally rabbit youngsters practice leaping into the air and chase each other around like wild. Since my dwarf rabbits get greens and fresh vegetables and fruits all year-round, the youngsters are also fed these foods right from the start. In addition, they get pellets with herbs, just like the adults. If baby rabbits couldn't tolerate greens, then wild rabbit offspring out in the meadow would have to grow up wearing muzzles.

After six weeks: The gastrointestinal tract of the young rabbits has now adjusted completely to solid food, even if they still nurse from their mother now and then.

At seven weeks: Depending on their stage of development, the youngsters can now be given up for adoption.

Teaching the youngsters to trust

In the beginning I check on the nest briefly every three days to make sure the babies are gaining weight. In the process, I get them used to my voice and my scent. If the little rascals leave the nest, I make the first cautious attempts at petting them. Later, in the exercise pen, I regularly lie down among them and coax the youngsters over with treats from my hand and a friendly tone of voice. At my house, the offspring also get used to other caregivers as well as all the noises associated with a household, such as the vacuum cleaner.

Two young bucks

▶ 1   **The Mini Lop** asserts his dominance over the younger dwarf. You can tell this by his posture and raised tail when they make nose contact.

▶ 2   **The dwarf** turns away. The Lop wants to inspect the dwarf's anal region. Soon he will no longer tolerate the younger rival in his territory.

◀ *It's easiest to communicate with your dwarf rabbits when they're at eye level with you.*

Hand-raising

You have to bottle-feed motherless kits. To do this, use lactose-reduced milk replacer for kittens or special colostrum (available from the veterinarian or at the pet store). Mix one part milk powder with two parts boiled water or diluted chamomile tea. Another milk recipe is two parts KMR plus one part Multimilk powder. Probiotic and infant multivitamin drops may be added. The milk temperature should be 96.8 to 100.4°F (36–38°C). Squirt the milk into the tiny mouth carefully so that the baby doesn't choke, at first with an oral syringe (without needle), then later with a nursing bottle. After each feeding, gently massage the kit's little belly with your fingers in the direction of the anus to stimulate digestion. Wipe away feces and urine with a tissue. Feed the kits about six times a day. Afterward, return them to their warm nest. The recommended daily amounts are as follows:

Newborns = 0.2 ounces (5 ml) 3 times daily and should be fed only milk until they are at least 10 days old;
Week 1 = 0.5 to 0.7 ounce (15 to 20 ml);
Week 2 = 0.8 to 0.9 ounce (25 to 27 ml);
Week 3 = 1 ounce (30 ml).
Add five drops of Sab Simplex to the daily milk ration to prevent intestinal gas.

MY PET

Do your rabbit babies differ from each other?

What I mean here is not the coat color, but rather the temperament of your little dwarf rabbits. By seven weeks the youngsters have developed to the point that you can recognize the first individual differences.

The test begins:
Observe the youngsters during their free-roaming time outside the cage:
○ Are there two who are especially fond of snuggling together? (Put them up for adoption as a pair!)
○ Is there one in the litter who is already chasing all the others around?
○ Who comes to you first when you coax them over?
○ Is one youngster more easily frightened than others by unfamiliar sounds?

My test results:

What to Do When There Are Problems

Dwarf rabbits are considered to be peaceable housemates. Most of the problems that arise when living with rabbits can be traced back to improper care by the owner.

Correcting Behavior Problems the Right Way

Even rabbits have their own idiosyncrasies and needs. If you understand the nature of these animals and know what they need as pets, then almost nothing will go wrong when you live together day in and day out. But sometimes misunderstandings do arise ...

Many of the rabbit's reactions may appear incomprehensible to us humans. Other behaviors can severely try our tolerance and patience. Suddenly you realize that "cuddly bunnies" are not always "cuddly."

Why Is My Rabbit Doing That?

Animals are complex, living creatures who behave as their nature dictates. Even if a rabbit is aggressive toward us on occasion, it would be wrong to accuse her of what would be considered "bad behavior" from our viewpoint. Many of the animals' so-called behavioral problems are, strictly speaking, problems caused by improper care by their human owners: No relief from the dreary monotony of life in a cage, no rabbit companions, or too little exercise are just a few examples. Other conflicts arise because we expect too much of our rabbits and demand that our little companions accommodate our needs. I'll describe below a few of the most common problems rabbit owners ask me about and suggest some solutions.

Wire Chewing

Situation 1: The rabbit chews and tugs on the wires of his cage while running back and forth excitedly. Meanwhile, another rabbit is running free outside his cage.
Cause: If this animal could talk, he would shout, "Let me out of here!"
What you can do: If you have to keep the rabbits separated for a while (see Neutering, page 85), place both cages close enough for the rabbits to see and sniff each other. So that both animals are still free to choose between staying in the cage and roaming free outside,

If a rabbit chews on the cage wires, he either wants out or is frustrated and bored.

Many dwarf rabbits suffer from **boredom** as pets, so make sure to provide plenty of activities for them.

divide the exercise area using wire fence panels. This way you can defuse a stressful situation and neither animal feels like a "prisoner."

Situation 2: The dwarf persists in chewing on the cage wires for no apparent reason.

Cause: This animal clearly has too little opportunity for activity and exercise.

What you can do: If your dwarf rabbit lives in a single-bunny household, I suggest you get another rabbit as a companion. Rabbits are naturally social and aren't really happy living alone. Another good idea would be to provide an interesting exercise area adjoining the cage where your pets could roam freely at any time. If this isn't always possible in your home, I suggest you get

_____

Timid, fearful rabbits often crouch for hours in their houses.

▼

a multilevel condo (see page 34). At least the animals could move around more there than in a simple one-room cage. To satisfy your rabbit's need to chew, provide a regular supply of twigs and untreated solid wood chews (see page 70).

The Timid Rabbit

Situation: The rabbit has lived in your household for several months, but is still timid and fearful whenever anyone approaches. She rarely comes out of her house, and during her free-roaming time she hides whenever someone enters the room. She doesn't like to be petted or held.

Cause: If this is a youngster who has exhibited this behavior right from the start, there are several possible causes: natural timidity of wild animals (hereditary), negative imprinting by a mother rabbit who was also timid and nervous, or being taken away from the mother too soon (before seven weeks of age). In addition, if a rabbit wasn't properly socialized or imprinted on humans when she was young, she'll have problems learning to trust given these unfavorable conditions (see Temperament, page 50). However, an older animal can have had an unhappy past, too, or maybe you made mistakes yourself in interacting with the rabbit.

What you can do: Take a closer look at the location you've chosen for the indoor cage (see page 35) and my suggested guidelines for getting along with your rabbit (see page 56). Avoid unnecessarily removing your bunny from the cage, carrying her around, and even petting her as long as she doesn't enjoy it. This would only increase the stress. Since many rabbits feel safer in an elevated home, a multilevel condo would be ideal (see page 34). Alternatively, you could place the cage on a low coffee table about 20 inches

the cage roof (on top only, not on the sides) to provide her with a little cover, though. This way, assisted by the above-mentioned measures, the fearful animal slowly learns to accept certain environmental stimuli.

Now begin offering your dwarf treats (her favorite greens and fresh foods) several times a day; holding them in your outstretched hand, slowly and

DID YOU KNOW THAT . . .

. . . rabbits can be aggressive?

In the wild, rabbits have to fight to defend their positions in the social hierarchy, their territory, their food sources, and their offspring. Mistakes made in raising and keeping them as pets often cause aggression in the animals. Rabbits can remember negative experiences quite well. Keep this in mind as you interact with them every day, because ridding a rabbit of bad habits is very difficult later on.

(50 cm) high. Once I simply shortened the legs of an old kitchen table. Then hang a ramp in the front door: 40 inches (100 cm) long, 8 inches (20 cm) wide. Cover the ramp with a coir mat or a carpet remnant so the rabbit can go up and down safely. This way your rabbit can hop in and out on her own whenever she likes and no longer has to put up with being grabbed. Now remove the nest box so the dwarf can't always retreat there and isolate herself from her environment. Lay a cloth over

carefully reach in through the front door of the cage. Stay at eye level with your pet and speak to her kindly so your fearful rabbit relaxes a bit and learns to think of you and your hand as something good. For best results, the rabbit should be hungry, but this doesn't mean there should be no hay or water in the cage. Don't lose patience or try to grab for the dwarf too soon and—if she's too afraid of your hand at first—set the treats down in front of her. Move away and try again from the

Billy the Bully

Our dwarf rabbit Billy is actually quite friendly. But in the last few weeks he has been attacking us as soon as we place his food bowl in the cage. My daughter no longer even dares to feed him. What can we do?

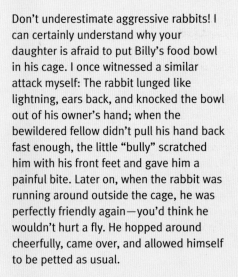

Don't underestimate aggressive rabbits! I can certainly understand why your daughter is afraid to put Billy's food bowl in his cage. I once witnessed a similar attack myself: The rabbit lunged like lightning, ears back, and knocked the bowl out of his owner's hand; when the bewildered fellow didn't pull his hand back fast enough, the little "bully" scratched him with his front feet and gave him a painful bite. Later on, when the rabbit was running around outside the cage, he was perfectly friendly again—you'd think he wouldn't hurt a fly. He hopped around cheerfully, came over, and allowed himself to be petted as usual.

Why is Billy acting like that?

Aggressive behavior in rabbits can have many causes. With your Billy, I suspect it's a case of so-called food-related aggression. Your rabbit seems to be quite dominant and defends his feeding area aggressively. There is nothing "abnormal" about this from the rabbit's point of view, but it should be remedied as soon as possible. As it now stands, Billy has learned that he achieves considerable success with his attacks. His humans retreat fearfully, and he can eat in peace.

Try this

First of all, get him to stop associating his feeding place with the need to defend his food. You've probably been placing his food bowl in the same spot in his cage all the time. From now on, feed your rabbit in a variety of places and sometimes in other forms. For instance, you can hang a veggie basket filled with greens and fresh foods from the roof of the cage, or do the same with twigs. Offer hay in a sock, or stick pelleted food in the cardboard tube from a roll of paper towels (see photos, pages 101 and 105). When your pet is roaming around outside his cage, keep changing the location of his food bowl in the exercise area. You and your daughter should also start hand-feeding your rabbit special treats outside the cage. I frequently hide food in boxes and tunnels, too, so that my animals have to work for it. With these measures, I hope Billy will soon be your daughter's beloved friend once more.

beginning later. It can take weeks, or even months, until the animal learns to trust you.

Sometimes "good examples" help as well. Once, when I took in a very timid doe who had been living alone in a small hutch, I let her run around in the pen together with my friendly rabbits. After she realized how the others received treats from my hand, she tried it herself one day. The doe still doesn't come over to me to be petted the way my other rabbits do, but on the other hand she snuggles all the more with her rabbit friends, and that's more important for a happy rabbit.

Inappropriate Elimination

In Chapter 6, page 100, I told you how you can train a rabbit to use a litter box. If problems persist, here are some helpful tips. Don't be disappointed, though: Not every house rabbit can be litter-box trained like an indoor cat. Some learn it almost by themselves, whereas others continue to have "accidents."

Age: Very young dwarf rabbits take a little longer to catch on at first. Their ability to learn and capacity for paying attention are still developing.

Castration: Bucks who had been litter-box trained begin to mark their territory when they become sexually mature. Castration at the appropriate time reduces this behavior (see page 85).

The wrong place: You have set up a litter box, but your dwarf continues to use his special corner. Put a second litter box in this spot. You should use something to block off other unwanted "latrines."

New Rabbits: If you introduce a second rabbit, your original rabbit might start marking his territory again temporarily. After the acclimation period, things usually return to normal.

Stress: If something upsets the animals and disrupts their happy home, this can also cause them to stop using their litter box. Try to think what's new or

Rabbits like to seek out concealed spots to do their business. You should put litter boxes in these places or else make them inaccessible. ▶

different now: a move, strangers in the house (substitute caretaker while you're on vacation), lengthy absence of someone important in their life, or even the loss of a bunny buddy. Try to restore that old familiar sense of well-being as soon as possible.

Health: If your rabbit has been using a litter box for a long time and now starts urinating elsewhere for no apparent reason, this could be because of a urinary tract infection, bladder stones, or other health problem. Take your bunny to the veterinarian.

Scaredy-cats and Roughnecks

In the ideal scenario, two littermates move into their new home together, are neutered at the appropriate time, receive proper care, and for the most part live together quite happily. In Chapter 3, page 58, you'll find suggestions for introducing a second rabbit to one that has been living alone. Here are some more tips for the "stubborn cases."

Declaration of war: The photos on this page show a brief but vigorous "exchange of blows" between two potent young bucks. Fighting over rank within the colony is a perfectly natural part of rabbit behavior, just like defending their territory (feeding place) and protecting their offspring. Rabbits can indeed be gentle, peaceful, cuddly, happy, and extremely social with each

2 **"Run for it!"** is the defeated Pumpkin's motto. But Mini Lop Freddy goes for him again, ears flying and tail raised.

▼

1 **The dominant** older Mini Lop Freddy is the clear victor in this altercation. With lightning speed he nips poor Pumpkin in the rump again as he tries to run away.

Uncastrated ("intact") bucks fight ▶
to establish social dominance.

other, but they are still rabbits and not "plush toys." Nevertheless, I want to encourage you not to give up right away if your rabbits fight. My two brawling bunnies (Pumpkin and Freddy) were castrated shortly after I took these photos and, after an acclimation period of about three weeks, were successfully integrated into my rabbit community.

The rivals are biting each other: Have you followed all the guidelines for introducing rabbits (see Neutering, page 85)? Despite everything, they don't just stop at chasing each other around harmlessly, even on neutral ground. The rabbits fight violently, biting and scratching until the fur flies. You most certainly have to intervene here. Interrupt the fight with a well-aimed squirt of water from a spray bottle. You can also try throwing a blanket over the combatants. I certainly wouldn't recommend that you try to break it up with your bare hands, though. Afterward put the two back in adjacent but separate cages to calm them down. Examine the rabbits for battle scars and injuries. Small bites can be easily treated with Swedish bitters or a wound ointment (see photo, page 90). For more severe injuries you must take your dwarf to the veterinarian.

Colony scent: Rub the newcomer with bedding from the cage of your original rabbit so that he doesn't smell so foreign (see page 19). As long as the two rabbits continue to behave aggressively, they should not be allowed to roam around outside the cage together without supervision. Take turns putting one of the animals in the other's cage, and keep the cages next to each other so the rabbits can see and sniff each other. Leave them in each other's cage overnight, then in the morning move them back. Switch them again the following night, and so on.

MY PET

Are you interested in documenting your dwarf rabbits?

If you think you've learned a lot about rabbit behavior by now, record it for yourself and other rabbit lovers. Take your camera and photograph your dwarfs.

Do this:

Put the photos on the Internet, write little stories to go along with them, and exchange ideas with other rabbit owners. Start your own rabbit diary. And here are a few more tips from me as a professional photographer: Never aim a flash directly at a rabbit's eyes. Stay at eye level with the animals. Try to keep the background as simple as possible. Use lenses that let you zoom in. Move carefully.

Enter your observations here:

More space: Although my rabbits have an area measuring 24 yard^2 (20 m^2) with plenty of places to run and hide, I open the door to create even more escape routes for them during the most intense period of adjustment. This way the subordinate rabbits can always avoid further fighting by running away. This is very important. Even in the wild, subordinate rabbits take to their heels and, although sometimes still pursued and harassed, manage to escape the worst attacks.

Fear, the tie that binds: Sometimes it helps to put your hooligans in a pet carrier (make sure no rabbit has marked it with his scent already) and drive them around in the car for about an hour. Or—as I have done—put all the dwarfs in a 12 yard^2 (10 m^2) backyard enclosure in the middle of the open lawn with no sort of shelter or place to hide. At first, it was stress for the rabbits, pure and simple, but it helped. The "battling bunnies" suddenly snuggled close together and forgot their quarrel. After that, things were much better at home.

Everything has its limits: Based on my own experience, I can tell you that I've been successful in introducing all my rabbits so far. Nevertheless, I do not advocate trying to force everything. If rabbits absolutely cannot stand each other, despite neutering, despite plenty of room, despite all your tricks, then you should respect this. In the long run, emotional stress leads to illness in animals as well as in us humans.

My Dwarf Has Run Away!

This happens more often than you might think. Before you know it, the little rascal has tunneled out of the pen, chewed through the chicken wire, or simply jumped over the fence. In Chapter 2, beginning on page 41, you learned how to avoid this. But hindsight, as everybody knows, is always better than foresight. So what can you do now?
Under no circumstance should you chase after the animal. In the first place, a dwarf rabbit is faster than you are, and in the second that would only make him panic and he could jump into a fence and hurt himself.
Instead, calmly and deliberately make a wide circle around the animal and then block his escape route simply by standing in front of him. If the rabbit tries to swerve to the left or right, simply step to that side. This way you can herd him back to the enclosure, because a rabbit will never charge you like a dog, but instead will instinctively turn away from you and hop back in the direction of his enclosure or hutch, i.e., to the safety of his burrow. If your rabbit has escaped into the neighbor's yard, don't assume that he will find his way back through the hole in the fence right away. In this case you can set up his familiar pet carrier and carefully try to coax him in. If the rabbit lies down on the ground, go up to him slowly, then kneel down and calmly pick up the "runaway." If your fugitive has already disappeared from sight, then it helps to

imagine how you would naturally behave in your rabbit's place. Your bunny is probably crouching somewhere in the high grass or under the bushes. You'll just have to search for him. If you still can't find your rabbit, you can only hope that he'll find his own way home by following his natural instincts. Just in case, you should leave both the cage and the enclosure open. In the meantime, any other rabbits living there should be safely confined elsewhere.

You can avoid food-related aggression by varying the feeding place.

Questions on
Behavior Problems

? When my doe Minnie had to go to the veterinary hospital for a few days, her cagemate Mickey attacked the poor thing as soon as she came back home. Didn't he recognize her anymore?

Your guess is not so far off. Minnie certainly smelled of strange people, anesthetics, and other upsetting things. Since rabbits communicate by scent and recognize each other by a shared colony scent, Mickey really didn't recognize Minnie as his old friend, but rather as an unfamiliar intruder who naturally had no business in his home. To prevent this, you can rub the "hospital rabbit" with a bit of bedding (straw) from home before returning her to the cage so that she smells familiar again. Or when you go to pick her up, put the rabbit who stayed home in the pet carrier and bring him along with you, then at the veterinarian's office put the little patient in with him. By the time you get home, she'll have her old familiar scent again.

? Recently my dwarf rabbit Fluffy was sitting in her litter box when the vacuum cleaner fell over as I was cleaning. Now my rabbit defecates in the exercise area outside her cage, something she never did before. Is there a connection?

Unfortunately, yes. Your Fluffy had a terrible shock and now she associates this with her litter box. Imagine that you were sitting on the toilet and lightning struck nearby. You'd certainly be in no hurry to return to this frightening place, either. My advice: Set up a second litter box, but try to make it as different as possible from the previous one. Keep putting your rabbit in it and reward Fluffy when she does her business there.

? My dwarf rabbit pair are allowed to roam freely in the house, since I have rabbit-proofed everything. The only thing I couldn't move out of reach was my heavy flowerpot with the 6-foot-tall palm. Of course, the rabbits jump in right there, dig in the dirt, and chew on everything. How can I prevent this?

If you can't remove the palm, you'll have to rabbit-proof the planter. Wrap some fine-mesh wire about 12 inches (30 cm) high around the planter and trunk. To let your indoor rabbits satisfy their passion for digging somewhere else, give them a roomy box filled with dirt or a mixture of dirt and sand. After all, rabbits just love to dig (see page 13).

(?) **My dwarf rabbit Snowflake is allowed to run loose in the children's room because she does her business in her cage like a good bunny. But yesterday, she jumped up on the bed and piddled on the pillow. Why is she doing that all of a sudden?**

Your rabbit has acclimated to living with you, but now she is older and has become a proper rabbit lady. And so it's only fitting that she mark such a lovely, cozy perch with her urine. It's as if she's saying, "This is my spot." I can only suggest that you protect the bed with a tarp in the future. If Snowflake jumps up, say, "No!" emphatically and clap your hands. If Snowflake obeys and hops down from the bed like a good rabbit, give her a treat. Try to give your rabbit a raised perch for her very own, as described on page 12, and hang a broad resting bench from the cage wires. You could also lay an old blanket on the cage roof where Snowflake can set up a lookout platform for herself.

(?) **My friend always takes care of my two rabbits when I go on vacation. For some reason, though, my animals don't like her. Could it be because my friend is so nervous and has a very shrill voice?**

If I were a rabbit, I wouldn't enjoy having this person around, either. Jumpy, nervous people frighten rabbits. A shrill voice is a constant irritation for those highly sensitive rabbit ears. Nothing against your dear friend, but if I were you, I would find a quiet, easygoing person to take care of your dwarf rabbits the next time you go on vacation.

(?) **Although my three rabbits are all castrated, I notice that they mount each other sometimes. What's the meaning of this odd behavior?**

This is a dominance gesture that one rabbit uses to show another who's boss. When the dominant animal mounts the other one and tries to mate with him, he is demonstrating his higher rank in the group. As long as it stays at that and the rabbits have arrived at an understanding, you shouldn't intervene.

Pet–sitter Information

Would you like to go on vacation and have a pet sitter look after your bunnies? Here you can write down everything your vacation substitute should know. This way, your dwarf rabbits will be well cared for, and you can relax and enjoy your vacation!

My dwarf rabbits' names are

This is what they look like:

This is what they like to eat:

this amount daily:

this amount once a week:

Occasional treats:

This is what they drink:

Proper feeding times:

Their food is stored:

Housekeeping:

This is cleaned every day:

This is cleaned once a week:

This is how they like to be petted:

Great activities for them:

They really dislike this:

My rabbits are not allowed to

This is also important:

Their veterinarian:

My address and phone number while I'm on vacation:

INDEX

ASSOCIATIONS AND CLUBS

American Rabbit Breeders Association, Inc.
P.O. Box 5667
Bloomington, IL 61702
Phone: (309) 664-7500
Fax: (309) 664-0941
E-mail: ARBAPOST@aol.com
www.arba.net/nationalclub.htm

American Dwarf Hotot Rabbit Club
Sharon Toon
4061 Tremont Ave.
Egg Harbor, NJ 08234
(609) 641-8839
stoon81611@aol.com

American Netherland Dwarf Rabbit Club
Sue Travis-Shutter
326 Travis Lane
Rockwall, TX 75032
(972) 771-4394
travisdwar@aol.com

Mini Lop Rabbit Club of America
Pennie Grotheer
P.O. Box 17
Pittsburg, KS 66762
(417) 842-3317
minilop@tiadon.com

National Mini Rex Rabbit Club
Doug King, Secretary
2719 Terrace Ave.
Sanger, CA 93657
(559) 787-2588
E-Mail: Kingsminirex@msn.com
http://www.nmrrc.com/

The North American Lionhead Rabbit Club
http://www.lionhead.us/

House Rabbit Society International Headquarters & Rabbit Center
148 Broadway
Richmond, CA 94804
Phone: (510) 970-7575
Fax: (510) 970-9820
www.rabbit.org

SCPA International
P.O. Box 0965
Wilton, NH 03086-9905
(866) 494-7722
www.spca.com

American Society for the Prevention of Cruelty to Animals (ASPCA)
424 E. 92nd St.
New York, NY 10128-6804
(212) 876-7700
www.aspca.org

Rabbit web resources:
http://netvet.wustl.edu/rabbits.htm

Finding a naturopathic veterinarian:

Academy of Veterinary Homeopathy
www.theavh.org

American Holistic Veterinary Medical Association
www.ahvma.org

Recommended Internet Addresses:

Everything you wanted to know about poisonous plants in the house and yard:

www.thegardenhelper.com/toxichouse.htm
www.hsus.org/pets/pet_care/protect_your_pet_from_common_household_dangers/common_poisonous_plants.html

Constructing enclosures:

www.rabbit.org/journal/1/place-space-update.html

MAGAZINES

Rabbits USA
Mission Viejo, CA
www.animalnetwork.com

BOOKS FOR MORE INFORMATION

Dieker, Andrea, and Jutta Steinkamp. *Dwarf Rabbits as a New Pet.* TFH Publications, 1992.

Gendron, Karen. *The Rabbit Handbook.* New York: Barron's Educational Series, Inc., 2000.

Harriman, Marinell. *House Rabbit Handbook: How to Live with an Urban Rabbit*, 4th ed. Alameda, CA: Drollery Press, 2005.

Kelsey-Wood, Dennis. *The Guide to Owning Dwarf Rabbits.* TFH Publications, 1998.

Leewood, Hazel. *Dwarf Rabbits (Pet Owner's Guide).* Lydney, UK: Ringpress Books, 2000.

Viner, Bradley. *All About Your Rabbit.* Hauppauge, NY: Barron's Educational Series, Inc., 1999.

Wegler, Monika. *Dwarf Rabbits (Complete Pet Owner's Manual),* Hauppauge, NY: Barron's Educational Series, Inc., 2008.

ACKNOWLEDG-MENTS

For reviewing the chapter on diseases and for their excellent care of my animals, I thank Dr. Hofstetter / Dr. Katikaridis, Wilhelm-Maigatter Weg 1, 85221 Dachau

The publisher and author also thank the firm of Pitti-Heimtierprodukte GmbH, Willich, for supplying the cages on pages 34 and 39 as well as the firm of Europet Bernina Int., Nürnberg, for providing the small-animal enclosures on pages 36, 40, and 46, as well as various cage furnishings.

Suppliers

www.ObiatOtto.de

Page 36: Rabbit Summer House

Page 44: Rabbit Hutch

THE PHOTOS

The illustrations on the front cover as well as the inside show the following:

Front cover: Young dwarf rabbit, agouti with white markings

Page 6: Mini Lop, five weeks old, dwarf rabbit, four weeks old

Page 32: Younger Mini Lop and dwarf rabbit in the suggested amphora

Page 48: Woman feeding dwarf rabbit

Page 62: Two dwarf rabbits, agouti with white markings

Page 75: Recommended hay rack, dwarf Munchkin with herb pot, two young dwarfs being hand-fed carrots

Page 76: Dwarf rabbit, orange and white, five weeks old

Page 96: Tricolor Mini Lop jumping over hurdle

Page 111: Hollow log, garden edging, leafy tent, willow trellis

Page 112: Mini Lop doe Minnie with her babies, five weeks old

Page 124: Red Netherland Dwarf Pumpkin chews up a carpet runner

Page 135: Mini Lop Freddy shreds scent-infused tissue, checks the anal region of a youngster, and mounts him (dominance mounting).

Important Tip

In dealing with rabbits, you can be injured if your rabbit scratches and bites. Have these injuries treated by a doctor. People with pet-hair allergies should consult a physician before getting a rabbit. To prevent life-threatening accidents with electricity, make sure that your dwarf rabbit cannot chew on any electrical cords.

The author and photographer

Monika Wegler has worked as a freelance photographer and author in Munich since 1983. She has illustrated more than 50 pet care handbooks, many of which she wrote herself. In addition to her books, she is well known for her calendars (Heye-Verlag), magazine articles, and advertising work. She has more than 20 years of practical experience in keeping and raising rabbits. Ms. Wegler raises rabbits, shares her home with them, and is well acquainted with animal rescue organizations, whose work she has supported actively and financially for many years. If you would like to learn more about the author and photographer, you can visit her home page: www.wegler.de.

All photographs in this handbook are hers, with the exception of page 7: Angermayer/Reinhard.

English translation © Copyright 2008 by Barron's Educational Series, Inc.

German edition by:
Monika Wegler

Published originally under the title *mein Zwergkaninchen*, in the series *mein Heimtier* © 2006 by Gräfe and Unzer Verlag GmbH, München

G|U

English translation by Mary D. Lynch

All inquiries should be addressed to:
Barron's Educational Series, Inc.
250 Wireless Boulevard
Hauppauge, New York 11788
www.barronseduc.com

ISBN: 978-0-7641-3712-9

Library of Congress Catalog Card No: 2007018992

Library of Congress Cataloging-in-Publication Data

Wegler, Monika.
  [Mein Zwergkaninchen. English]
  My dwarf rabbit / Monika Wegler ; translation from the German by Mary D. Lynch.
    p. cm.—(My pet)
  Includes bibliographical references.
  ISBN-13: 978-0-7641-3712-9 (alk. paper)
  ISBN-10: 0-7641-3712-3 (alk. paper)
  1. Dwarf rabbits.   I. Title.

SF455.D85W43713 2008
636.932'2—dc22

                                    2007018992

Printed in China
9 8 7 6 5